CHRIST IS ALL

D0886504

LESLIE HARDINGE

Pacific Press Publishing Association
Boise, Idaho
Oshawa, Ontario, Canada

To
Molly
my best friend
whose life has shown me for
almost sixty years that
Christ Is All
this book is
dedicated

Edited by Don Mansell
Designed by Tim Larson
Cover by photos by Duane Tank
Type set in 10/12 Century Schoolbook

The author assumes full responsibility for the accuracy of the citations and references appearing in this book.

Library of Congress Card Catalog Number: 88-61590

ISBN 0-8163-0785-7

88 89 90 91 92 · 5 4 3 2 1

Contents

Studies in the Book of Leviticus

Introduction to Leviticus

Many translations call Leviticus the "Third Book of Moses." Our English name comes from the Greek and means "the Levitical book," although Levites are mentioned only a few times.[1] The reason is that it contains rules by which the Levites carried out their ministrations. The Hebrews remember the book by its opening words, "and He called."

While Moses laid no claim to authorship, the phrase, "The Lord spake unto Moses," or the like, occurs more than fifty times. The Saviour has decided the matter by recognizing Moses as the author on several occasions.[2]

These regulations clarified the ways in which God's people had been worshiping Him from the beginning and are replete with symbols and types of salvation. The book of Hebrews describes these laws as "shadows of good things to come" and focuses them on the activities of Christ. Ellen White has recommended this approach: "We should show them that the Old Testament is as verily the gospel in types and shadows as the New Testament is in its unfolding power. The New Testament does not present a new religion; and the Old Testament does not present a religion to be superseded by the New. The New Testament is only the advancement and unfolding of the Old. The gospel is given in precept in Leviticus."[3]

Leviticus lies at the heart of the Pentateuch, and without it the ministry of Christ would be shrouded in mystery. Through its representations the Saviour is revealed as working within a timetable.[4] By His rituals He daily cleanses His people, and eventually His sanctuary, and thus ensures their holiness, and,

5

at the consummation of His redemptive work, proclaims a Jubilee. A study of Leviticus confirms that Christ is indeed all!

Genesis pictures the road down which mankind stumbled from Eden, while Exodus shows God redeeming His elect from bondage and leading them by fire and cloud toward the Promised Land. In Leviticus, Jehovah teaches His people that access to Him is through blood ministered by His appointed priest. The types of Exodus are prophetic of Christ the Redeemer, while those of Leviticus focus on the worship of God through Christ the Sacrifice and Priest. The objective of the book is holiness.

There are forty references to Leviticus in the New Testament, and all are types. If it were not for this book we should have little idea of our High Priest's ministry, especially on the antitypical day of atonement.

Part I
Sacrifices and Offerings
Preview

The sanctuary offerings illustrate Christ's sufferings[1] and the way He atones for the sinner. Three characteristics are basic to all sacrifices: (i) the offerer, (ii) the offering, and (iii) the priest, and the focus throughout is on Jesus. Because He is many things, and fills many roles, many symbols are needed to portray Him.

Jesus is the ultimate Offering, hanging on the altar of the cross as the representative of man and his kinsman, presenting himself to God on his behalf.[2] Since guilty man has nothing with which to pay his debt, the Saviour cancels it with His life. The rituals display the penitent's part as identifying with the offering, and thus being "accepted in the beloved." [3]

Jesus is the ultimate Offering, assuming the position of man condemned under the law, showing that "as he is, so are we in this world."[4] On that dateless date when Deity agreed that Jesus should come to this earth as man's example and substitute, the Saviour promised in the councils of heaven, "Lo, I come: in the volume of the book it is written of me, I delight to do thy will, O my God: yea, thy law is within my heart."[5] As Mary's Baby He assumed the body "prepared" or "fitted" for Him,[6] and, as the Offering, He gave it up to die "for us."[7] In life and death He sets mankind the example, and as their Substitute, perished for humanity.

Since the sacrifices represented the holy Jesus, they must be without "spot, or wrinkle, or any such thing."[8] Because Christ is our Creator, He was entitled to pay man's ransom. From His redeemed ones He wants, not cruel sacrifices,[9] but obedience and

7

mercy from a loving heart.[10] This He fully exemplified, affirming, "I delight to do thy will, O my God."

Jesus is the ultimate Priest, illustrated by Israel's mediators. But only after the victim had been slain, could the high priest take its "spilled blood" to where the sinner longed to go. After Calvary, Christ entered the heavenly sanctuary to serve. And on the antitypical day of atonement took His "spilled blood" into the most holy place, and there with His "sprinkled blood" made atonement for every penitent.

Christ embraces every one of His sons and daughters within Himself and is thus able to present them to God in the heavenly sanctuary as the Offerer, the Offering, and the Priest, and then claim His victory on their behalf. These truths are revealed in every sacrifice. In each offering we should look for (i) man's view of Christ's sacrifice, (ii) God's view of Christ's sacrifice, and (iii) God's view of man's sacrifice in Christ.

Three elements bring about purification in the sanctuary ritual: blood, water, and fire.

Blood cleanses from sin.[11] "It is the blood that maketh an atonement for the soul" because "the life of the flesh is in the blood."[12] Blood symbolizes a life laid down in sacrifice and is therefore precious. In some rituals blood was represented by wine, the essence of the grape.

Water removes superficial defilement easily and painlessly and points to the "fountain . . . for sin and for uncleanness" that flowed from the riven heart of Christ.[13] Paul compared the inspired word applied to the believer's mind by the regenerating Spirit to this water [14] penetrating the "joints and marrow,"[15] and illustrated by baptism.[16] Ritual blood and ritual water combine to make the sacrifice efficacious.[17]

For destroying defilement, no finer agent exists than fire, a type of one function of the Holy Spirit. Through His fire Jehovah purges the dross from the sinner.[18] The altar fire came from God[19] and symbolized His acceptance of what was worthy.

Chapter 1

The Whole Burnt Offering

All I *am* is Christ's

"When the burnt offering began, the song of the Lord began also."[1] God provided the Sacrifice, and Israel praised, his heart inspired to sing because of the Gift on the altar. Calvary has turned man's sadness to joy and spread anthems across the far-flung universe. When morning stars sang in ecstasy, the Father's voice was hushed. When angels caroled the birth of His son, His Father was silent still. But when Satan's furnace roared on Golgotha and the accepting fires of Divine love consumed the Victim on the altar cross, the Father's song of exultation began; His kingdom was forever safe!

The burnt offering was a "gift,"[2] a willing pledge of dedication by individuals or the whole nation. Its Hebrew name,[3] meaning "what ascends," suggests an "offering which reaches up to God." A further designation suggesting "whole"[4] adds the idea of completeness.[5] The Septuagint and the Vulgate both use a word which has come into English as *holocaust*, something burned up. The Hebrew root for *incense*, to smolder fragrantly, when applied to the burnt offering, describes it as reaching up to heaven as a "sweet savor" or "satisfying odor." Inspiration employs these five word pictures to alert the worshiper to aspects of the burnt offering consumed on the altar, yet, rising up to Heaven as a fragrant gift on perfumed wings of loving sacrifice, as did Mary's spikenard.[6]

The Lord permitted six kinds of victims: tame and docile oxen, sheep and goats, and domestic and wild birds, turtle-doves, pigeons, and occasionally sparrows[7]. As he made his selection, the worshiper considered the qualities of the creature which was to die in his place. "The strength of the ox"[8] bearing burdens[9] typified Him who, as the "firstling" of a bull[10], patiently toiled in sacrificial service. The gentle ram whispered of the uncomplaining One who was "brought as a lamb to the slaughter"[11] to provide His skin to cover the sinner's nakedness.[12] The vigorous goat recalled the sin-offering bearing mankind's guilt. And in pastel pigments pigeons painted the portrait of the "harmless" One,[13] mourning "as a dove"[14] over human indifference, clawed to death by cruel fingernails.[15] "Sold for a farthing" and cast aside,[16] the sparrow identified Him who was "despised and esteemed not," yet cheerfully came to dwell under the eaves of human habitations.

The characteristics of each creature were lenses through which the worshiper looked into the nature of Jesus. He chose the victim that best expressed his understanding of the burnt offering, but economics must also have played a role. The Lord allowed the penitent to present whatever substitute he was able to obtain as a burnt offering.

The burnt offering was the earliest ritual mentioned in the Bible. The law emphasized sixteen times that no rite was to displace it and all other sacrifices must be in addition to "the continual burnt-offering." Slain for centuries each morning and evening in the sanctuary as the heart of Israel's "daily" services, this offering emphasized the need for regular personal and congregational consecrations to God.[17]

The Spirit first moves the sinner to repent and then induces him to adore.[18] His heart, aglow with gratitude and love for his Saviour, burns for expression. Words seem inadequate to display his joy and affirm his resolve to amend, and the penitent longs to do something in appreciation. Jehovah devised the burnt offering to satisfy these deep yearnings and meet this need to present a gift. While selecting his stand-in, the worshiper clung to God's promise, "it will be accepted on his behalf."[19]

Since the burnt offering represented the perfect Redeemer, and only secondarily the sinner, he must find the best "clean"[20] animal or bird "without blemish"[21] available to him. Even the archfiend could find "nothing"[22] wrong with God's great Sacrifice. A bruise or defect, excessive or wanting part disqualified the victim.

The burnt offering was to be presented without compulsion. With his heart filled with love, the penitent was to give the Lord his choicest offering. See the Saviour in this, yielding His body to serve as His Father should direct, and laying down His life as the sinner's ransom. Only willing surrender must drive the penitent to lay himself down as "a living sacrifice,"[23] and this alone enabled him to approach God's ideal and "be perfect to be accepted."[24]

Accompanied by the priest, the worshiper led his substitute to the "door of the tabernacle," or entry veil to the holy place. There he found the spot, northward of the altar,[25] that is, north of an imaginary line running east and west through the center of the court and tabernacle, where stakes were fixed.[26] To one of these he tethered the animal "with cords."[27] When the court was crowded, he might temporarily bind the victim to "the horns of the altar."[28]

The sinner then tied the animal's legs together so that it fell on its side, with its face toward the sanctuary. He "put" "both" his hands[29] upon its head to signal the transference of his sin. The verb pictures him leaning his weight upon the creature. Imagine a lamb crushed beneath a man's weight, and then envision the Lamb of God as He "fell"[30] beneath the load of human guilt in Gethsemane and was pinned under His cross on the Vía Dolorosa.[31] In this way the sinner obeyed the Spirit's invitation to cast "all your care upon him; for he careth for you."[32]

With hands symbolically pressing his guilt upon the victim's head, and facing the most holy place, the penitent silently confessed his sins and pledged amendment in the ancient prayer which concluded with the words, "I return in repentance, and let this be for my atonement [covering]."[33] He believed that his substitute had taken responsibility for his "past" sins.[34] Observe this road to faith, and roll[35] your burdens upon your Sacrifice.

The sinner then grasped the knife and slit the victim's throat,[36] acknowledging that his sin caused his proxy's death. He accepted the claim of God's law, agreeing that death resulted from transgression, and affirmed that his only escape was through the sacrifice of the One who would one day take his place. In your mind's eye gaze on the sinner's knife held to the victim's throat and acknowledge that we, too, slay the Son of

God, that our voices join the obscene chant, "Crucify Him! Crucify Him!"

Should a bird be presented, "the priest shall bring it unto the altar" and pinch off the head with his nail,[37] pluck off its feathers, and fling them on the ashes piled by the east of the altar. Squeezing its tiny body, he smeared the sides of the altar with its blood. Then taking the knife, he cut open its carcass to expose its heart before salting and laying it on the altar.

This pictures the Priest-Victim taking Himself to Calvary with the pledge, "I lay down my life" for you.[38] For fifteen centuries this cruel rite anticipated the horror of Christ's priestly duty in offering Himself. Neither God nor demon compelled Him to step from His throne and tramp to old Skullface. There the Victim-Priest deliberately shed His own life's blood that we might comprehend the depths of His love.

The animal was hung from hooks affixed in frames provided in the court,[39] and there the offerer flayed it, presenting its pelt to the priest.[40] This sings of the proto-gospel: "Unto Adam also and to his wife did the Lord God make coats of skins, and clothed them."[41] The "covering" of the murdered Lamb provides the robe to conceal the nakedness of sin. The "fine linen" glistens with the righteousness of Christ to form the material from which He makes the trousseau for His repentant bride.[42]

The sharpened blade had a further task. "He shall cut [the victim] into his pieces."[43] God "commanded" a precise technique for dissecting the sacrifices.[44] And so the knife dismembered the carcass in the manner required by law.[45] Finally the heart was cut open to release the blood. See Jesus in this act. Pierced by the Roman lance, the "fountain . . . for sin and for unrighteousness"[46] gushed forth. The fat or suet, suggesting beauty, magnificence, or preciousness, was removed from its "inwards," and the entire creature, in Paul's expression, possibly borrowed from this ritual, rightly divided.[47]

The offerer bathed the "inwards" and the "legs" in water ladled from the laver and dried them with towels. These parts might symbolize inner thoughts and outward walk, and their cleansing directs us to the sinless Saviour and His goal for all penitents. The gospel "laver" is the word of God.[48] When the believer decides to place himself as a "living sacrifice" on the altar, the Spirit uses the "water" of the word to cleanse the inner secrets of his mind, as well as his outward conduct.

"The sinew which shrank" was flung on the heap of ashes gathered at the east of the altar.[49] Cut from each back leg, it might neither be eaten nor offered. This tendon recalled Jacob's defeat and victory at Jabbok,[50] and suggested that God wanted nothing flawed placed on His altar.

The priest caught the blood spurting from the dying victim in a silver vessel and carried it up the ramp to the platform, or "compass," around the altar.[51] Moving to its north-eastern corner, he sprinkled some of it on its eastern and northern sides. Walking around this ledge to its south-western corner, he repeated this act on the altar's western and southern sides.[52] The residue he emptied at the base of the altar to form its symbolic foundation.

Only the priest might apply sacrificial blood. The Lord explained, "The life of the flesh is in the blood: and I have given it to you upon the altar to make an atonement for your souls: for it is the blood that maketh atonement for the soul."[53] The word *atonement* literally means "to cover up."[54] When Wycliffe translated the Hebrew as "at-one-ment," he described the results of this rite.

In imagination join with the Revelator in watching Jesus, both Victim and Priest, spilling His blood in Gethsemane and on Golgotha, and then ascending to His Father in triumph. See the veil of the celestial sanctuary lifted, and gaze at God's throne in the most holy place where the bleeding Lamb is paying His blood as the price of redemption.[55] The flock of God is ransomed by the Shepherd's death. Rejoice!

The victim's dismembered and washed parts were salted by the priest. "In the ritual service, salt was added to every sacrifice. This . . . signified that only the righteousness of Christ could make the service acceptable to God. Referring to this practice, Jesus said, 'Every sacrifice shall be salted with salt.' 'Have salt in yourselves, and have peace one with another [Mark 9:49, 50].' All who present themselves a 'living sacrifice, holy, acceptable unto God' (Rom. 12:1), must receive the saving salt, the righteousness of our Saviour."[56] Since salt inhibits decay, "the Spirit . . . is compared to salt, because of its preserving

qualities."[57] "The savor of the salt is divine grace"[58] and symbolizes the Spirit's ministry which flavors every aspect of life and
establishes the "covenant of salt."[59] In biblical times those who
ate food containing salt surrendered any enmity they might have
cherished against their host and pledged loyalty. These salted
portions, the "food" of the altar,[60] were "eaten" by the "consum-
ing fire," assuring the participants of fellowship with Heaven.

The head, fat, legs, and "inwards" were consumed by the
flames.[61] Head represents man's will and thoughts, while legs
tell of his daily walk, his life's direction. "Inwards" [kidneys and
liver] whisper of emotions and secret longings, while fat adds
overtones of well-being.[62] To "eat the fat of the land"[63] meant to
enjoy the best it had.

These four parts of the offering symbolize the fullness of
Christ's consecration. His teaching sums up this dedication:
"Thou shalt love the Lord thy God with all thy heart, and with
all thy soul, and with all thy mind."[64] The antitypical Burnt Of-
fering clearly displayed this attitude by giving Himself totally to
His Father,[65] and "as he is, so are we in this world."[66]

The priest took the washed and salted portions, and flung
them upon the burning fig wood logs he had laid "in order"
on the grate of the altar.[67] Picking up a flesh hook, he grouped
these disarranged pieces into the semblance of the creature's
form. Sing! This acted parable is the spring of peace and hope.
When the disciple first casts himself on God's altar, his life often
seems confused. But wait! Our Priest is in control. In His good
time He will bring "order"[68] out of our jumbled experiences.

The sacred altar fire had been ignited by God Himself at
Sinai, and the priests were to ensure that it never went out.
They did this in the wilderness by adding incense to a censer of
coals they carried on the march.[69] These embers kindled the
altar wood, and from it sprang the sparks which lighted all the
sacred fires used throughout the sanctuary. The Lord's message
is clear: the incense of prayer must keep alight the flame of God's
love on the censer of our hearts throughout life's wanderings.

The rabbis remembered that while the logs for the altar might
be obtained from any tree "save only olive-wood and the wood of
the vine," "their custom was to use only boughs of the fig-tree or
walnut-tree or of oleaster-wood."[70] In Scripture the fruitless

fig tree, the first choice, is used as an illustration of hypocrisy.[71] The gospels note that nothing "burned" the Lamb of God quite as fiercely as did Pharisaic self-righteousness!

Watch the flame feed on each part of the victim until only ashes remains. Fire portrays an aspect of Deity which accepts and consumes. His flame ratified Abel's offering and approved Elijah's sacrifice, but also warned of the lake of death in which Sodom drowned. The alternatives are clear: either the heavenly fire consumes the substitute bearing his confessed sins, or the sinner perishes with his guilt.

The ascending smoke gave evidence of the holocaust, while the ashes proclaimed, "It is finished!" God's justice had accepted the victim, and His love was satisfied. These ashes looked forward to the "fulness of the time"[72] when Heaven's Sacrifice will have paid redemption's price to "the uttermost farthing."[73] See this act in the bruised and bleeding Victim hanging on the cruel tree, until His cry "Into thy hands I commend my spirit" marked the moment He cast Himself into His Father's arms.[74] An understanding of the burnt offering removed the fear of punishment and assured the penitent of his acceptance "in the beloved."[75]

Following His resurrection, the Saviour ascended to heaven, to hear from His Father's lips that His sacrifice was accepted, and then returned to comfort His disciples for forty days. The verbs describing His ascent, "going up"[76] and "carried up"[77] are the very ones used in the Greek Old Testament to picture the results of the burning. As the worshiper observed the smoke ascending to heaven with "the sparks [that] fly upward,"[78] he believed that he was accepted by God.

The Lord evaluated this rite as "a sweet savour."[79] The Hebrew means "rest"[80] and recalls the Creator's satisfaction at His perfected task.[81] It suggests the fulfillment of a bride and groom married in love,[82] and anticipates the joy of the redeemed in eternal fellowship with Christ the Bridegroom.[83] When the perfume of Calvary's Burnt Offering reached Heaven, the Father was delighted with all that was purchased by His Holocaust. This odor proclaimed, "Christ also hath loved us, and hath given himself for us an offering and sacrifice to God for a sweetsmelling savour."[84] And as Jesus sees the souls saved as the result of the "travail of his soul," He, too, will be "satisfied."[85]

The most dramatic burnt offering in Old Testament history was the one which God commanded Abraham to sacrifice. "Take now thy son, thine only son Isaac, whom thou lovest, and get thee into the land of Moriah; and offer him there for a burnt offering."[86] The only claim to fame of the "friend of God"[87] was that he had a son by Sarah. What else had he achieved? He wrote no book; he built no city. Had he failed in bringing up a son, Abraham's accomplishment would have been little. In complying with the Divine order to kill his son, he was actually destroying the very essence of his existence. The knife on Mount Moriah would end everything.

In his act of offering up Isaac, Abraham reached the point at which, for all intents and purposes, Isaac was dead. In his mind he had slaughtered his son, and now there was nothing he could do about the descending blade. At that moment the angel held his hand. Abraham's total dedication displayed the scope of the burnt offering. And then, because of the substitute ram caught in a crown of thorns,[88] doomed Isaac was spared. Christ focused the patriarch's memorable deed and Isaac's "living sacrifice" of himself on "my day."[89] It was a tableau of what the Father and His only Son were to do on Calvary, near the very spot at which Isaac had been sacrificed. In Israel's ritual the burnt offering represented the penitent's gift of his own life as a "living sacrifice" in full surrender to the Divine mandate, and by this act of devotion declared, "All I *am* is Christ's."

Chapter 2

The Meal/Drink Offerings

All I *have* is Christ's

God required a cereal offering, with olive oil and grape juice, to accompany every burnt offering and every peace offering.[1] He had not insisted on this in the wilderness, as the people had only manna.[2] But in the Promised Land this offering was a "present"[3] in appreciation for life's material blessings, and given to say, "Thank You!" to God. The Hebrew name, *mincah*,[4] first occurs in the story of Cain and Abel[5] and came from a root meaning to appease or satisfy. Its significance is illustrated by Jacob's present to Esau[6] and that of the ten brothers to Joseph.[7] Modern translators have rendered it grain or cereal offering.

Since man was originally a tiller of the soil, the fruit of his labor constituted his wealth, and from it he brought offerings to his bountiful Creator. The cereals from which he made his selections were barley, spelt, goat grass, oats,[8] and sometimes rice.[9] These helpful grasses, lacking the majesty of the cedar or the loveliness of the orchid, the strength of the oak or the longevity of the sequoia, provide man and other creatures with daily bread. Wheat flour was the first choice, as the rabbis affirm, "fine-flour . . . is the special sense of the term 'Meal-offering.' "[10]

Ponder the acted parable illustrating the "cruelty" connected with bread making. Man's share cuts a grave in the earth, into which he flings the "corn of wheat" to lie and die in darkness.[11] Heaven's sun and rain vivify the germ, and the seed springs up, "first the blade, then the ear, after that the full corn in the ear."[12] "In the fullness of time" man's sickle cuts off their heads, and his flails thrash them unmercifully, for "bread corn is bruised"[13] until the gale drives off the chaff.

17

The miller crushes the grist between his stones, and sifts the meal "through thirteen sieves,"[14] until it is free from all unevenness. Like its Antitype, the grain offering was presented with every preparation completed. This "fine flour," as the life essence of the cereal, illustrated man's best efforts, his work and worth, and was a prophetic type of Jesus.

But should the worshiper decide to make the flour into bread, strong hands kneaded and pummeled its substance, and the oven's fire raged against the dough to mature the loaf. These acts picture what the Bread of Life suffered[15] as, beaten and bruised, He patiently submitted to man's inhumanity.

Oil[16] from crushed ripe olives was part of every meal offering. The rabbis recall that "the cakes required to be mingled [with oil], and the wafers to be anointed. How did they anoint them? In the form of [a cross like the Greek letter] chi."[17] This cruciform chrism sang a prophetic song: "God anointed Jesus of Nazareth with the Holy Spirit and with power."[18] Watch how He directed the Saviour before His birth,[19] moment by moment throughout His life, and in His death and resurrection,[20] and we see how He helped Him to become man's perfect Meal-offering.

The Israelite was to present God with the harvest of his life's activities, softened and flavored with the oil of the Spirit.[21] His holy presence hallows, making the worshiper a "partaker of the divine nature."[22] Then day by day His power imparts grace to enable the disciple to fulfill the divine ideal.[23]

Salt was mingled with the meal offering during its preparation,[24] and its antiseptic properties preserved it from corruption. This symbol represented the flavoring and preserving influence of the Spirit.

Frankincense, as part of every meal-offering,[25] contributed fragrance. The Hebrew word for this aromatic gum suggests whiteness, and from its root sprang the name of the snow-crowned Lebanon Mountains. As its spiced smoke rose to God, it enhanced the cereal offering and covered the acrid smell of the burning flesh of the victim, while its color reminded the worshipers of the purity of the Messiah. In incense the frankincense symbolized "the merits and intercession"[26] of our immaculate Saviour, whose fragrant priestly mediation renders man's offerings acceptable to God.[27]

But salt is valueless until it mingles with the dough and is lost to sight, and frankincense remains inert until it is consumed by the flame. Oil and frankincense together tell of the gladness and sweetness of Jesus which render man's gifts pleasing to the Father,[28] while the salt imparts the constancy of the Spirit's keeping presence.

"No grain offering . . . shall be made of anything that ferments,"[29] the Lord warned, and so leaven of all kinds was excluded from the altar. Yeast or leaven is the force behind fermentation and is the symbol of any principle which works from within to transform, and when honey is added, the process is facilitated.[30] And so honey was also prohibited.[31] Bible students have compared its cloying and sickening sweetness[32] with the lusts of the flesh, at first pleasing, but eventually destructive to the spiritual life.[33] In this prohibition against leaven and honey God showed His desire for "the harvests" of man's endeavors to be presented unadulterated and from a sincere heart.

But should the grateful farmer bring "first-fruits" to show his appreciation, he might present both leaven and honey with the fresh ears.[34] Did this suggest the Lord's readiness to accept any spontaneous acts of loving gratitude, whatever the motive?

In each of the three ways for preparing the meal offering the dough must be "kneaded in lukewarm water, and care was needed lest [it] become leavened."[35] "Living water" points to the refreshing, softening ministry of the Saviour's love.[36] With oil and salt added, the dough was pressed into flat cakes similar to Indian chapatis or Mexican tortillas.

In the first method the "cake" was perforated to prevent its puffing up and was called "pierced bread."[37] Long before His ordeal on old Skullface Jesus had prophetically cried, "My heart is wounded [pierced] within me."[38] As they presented meal offerings the perceptive Israelites might "look upon [Him] whom they have pierced."[39]

The oven used is also translated "furnace"[40] and pictures the affliction Christ bore. David wrote of the wicked, "Thou shalt make them as a fiery oven in the time of thine anger."[41] Because He also survived the flaming darts flung by *diabolos*, literally the "one who throws through,"[42] Jesus became the perfect "pierced Bread."

In the second method thin wafers were cut into pieces, suffused with oil, and cooked on a griddle.[43] The Hebrew word for *wafer* means "to flail or pound," and suggest other kinds of suffering borne by our Saviour.

In the third method the cake was prepared in a frying pan.[44] *Frying* means "bubbling up in heat."[45] Rabbi Gamaliel noted that "a frying-pan is deep and what is cooked therein is spongy, while the baking-pan is flat and what is cooked thereon is solid."[46]

The different ways legislated for cooking the *mincah* apparently show how the fire reached the dough. In the oven the wafer was surrounded by heat. This passed through the griddle to touch the heart of the cake. In the frying pan the hot oil pervaded the *mincah*. Did these techniques picture the myriad "fiery trails" which Heaven's Meal Offering endured in His preparation for His Father's altar table?

The fresh ears of the first fruits were simply parched by the fire, and the grain "beaten out."[47] Was this act to alert the worshiper to the stripes of the One by whom every sinner might be healed?[48]

With the admixture of oil, salt, and frankincense the cakes were brought to the altar.[49] The priest's first act was to elevate a "memorial" portion to call God's attention to the offerer[50] before he burned it upon the burnt offering or peace offering already smoldering on the altar. The remainder of the *mincah* he took home for his family's use.[51] When the offering consisted simply of fine flour he took a handful, not too full, and not too empty, the rabbis warn,[52] and with the salt and frankincense, burned it as a "memorial." The remainder was his perquisite. Should the offering be a cake, it was treated as were the others.[53] The smoke arising from the *mincah* reached Jehovah as a "sweet smelling savor," bringing satisfaction to His heart.

Since meal offerings belonged to the four "most holy things",[54] they were eaten by the priest and his family "in a holy place." This was originally "the court of the tabernacle," but was interpreted by later Judaism as any location within the walls of Jerusalem.[55] This "eating" pictured identification.

The Lord required *mincahs* with every burnt offering and every peace offering in quantities determined by the types of sacrifices they accompanied. This was to teach that the products of man's efforts were acceptable solely on the basis of the spilled blood. In every age the Crucified One alone has added worth to the works of man.

Today "religious services, the prayers, the praise, the penitent confession of sin ascend from true believers as incense to the heavenly sanctuary; but passing through the corrupt channels of humanity, they are so defiled that unless purified by blood, they can never be of value with God. They ascend not in spotless purity, and unless the Intercessor who is at God's right hand presents and purifies all by His righteousness, it is not acceptable to God. All incense from earthly tabernacles must be moist with the cleansing drops of the blood of Christ. He holds before the Father the censer of His own merits, in which there is no taint of earthly corruption. He gathers into this censer the prayers, the praise, and the confession of His people, and with these He puts His own spotless righteousness. Then, perfumed with the merits of Christ's propitiation, the incense comes up before God wholly and entirely acceptable. Then gracious answers are returned.

"O that all may see that everything in obedience, in penitence, in praise and thanksgiving must be placed upon the glowing fire of the righteousness of Christ. The fragrance of this righteousness ascends like a cloud around the mercy seat."[56]

The significance of this teaching of the *mincah* is illustrated by the story of Cain and Abel. Ignoring this divine requirement, Cain presented only the products of his husbandry, while Abel obediently brought his burnt offering as well as[57] his meal offering.[58] The Lord used the same word to describe Abel's *mincah* as He did Cain's, and there is no reason to apply *mincah*, as some wish to do, to Abel's animal sacrifice, which is specifically mentioned separately. Because Cain's meal offering lacked the base of the burnt offering it was rejected. And since Abel also brought a burnt offering, his *mincah* was accepted. The rabbis' warning that "if the bread offering is brought without the lambs, there is naught that renders it permissible"[59] is a significant comment on this ancient story.

"When Abel offered the firstling of the flock, he acknowledged God, not only as the Giver of his temporal blessings [recognized by his *mincah*], but also as the Giver of the Saviour [typified by the blood of the slain animal]. Abel's gift was the very choicest he could bring; for it was the Lord's specified claim. But Cain brought only of the fruit of the ground, and his offering was not accepted by the Lord. It did not express faith in Christ. All our offerings must be sprinkled with the blood of the atonement [therefore Abel's *mincah* must have been touched with the blood of his burnt offering]. As the purchased possession of the Son of God, we are to give the Lord our own individual lives."[60]

The sacrificial victim represented the dedicated celebrant and looked ahead to his Substitute, while the *mincah* pictured the harvest of human endeavor, as well as "the fruits of the Spirit" developed within the human personality. Through His condemnation of Cain, God showed that He would not accept man's material offering until he had first placed himself on the altar as a "living sacrifice." By his burnt offering the worshiper affirmed, "All I *am* is Christ's," and then on the basis of this dedication, further declared through his meal offering, "All I *have* is Christ's."

The Lord required a libation as accessory of every meal offering,[61] explaining, "The drink offering thereof shall be of wine."[62] The rabbis add the following information, "No fruit juice is offered on the altar excepting the produce of olives and grapes."[63] Some Bible students have thought that meal offerings and drink offerings were independent of each other. But the truth is that whenever a meal offering was prescribed, a drink offering was understood to be necessary as well, and vice versa. For example, the Mishna reminds us that "all the offerings of an individual or the congregation require drink offerings," and the editor Herbert Danby adds, "Meal offerings are here also intended."[64]

And because of this the chalice was filled with "the pure blood of the grape,"[65] and the libation poured over its burnt offering as well as its peace offering, and the "memorials" of other cereal offerings[66] being consumed on the altar. As "a sacrifice made by fire" the wine, the very substance of the grape, played a vital part. The Hebrew verb *nasak*, from which the word "drink offering" *nesek*, was derived means to pour a liquid out[67] or over[68] something, and so came to mean "to cover over," and thus "to protect."[69]

Drink offerings were never drunk. In fact, God pronounced an anathema against any one who drank them[70] or ate blood. Ritual wine typified blood and pointed to the Messiah's perfect life poured out by the wine press of God's wrath. The ban against drinking ritual wine paralleled the Lord's prohibition against eating blood.[71]

Like bread making, the production of wine is full of "cruel" imagery. First the vine was so drastically pruned that it appeared dead. Then when the grapes ripened, man ruthlessly cut them off with his knife and flung them into the wine press. There he trampled upon them till the crimson juice flowed freely. How vividly the expression "the blood of grapes"[72] anticipates the carmine extract of the fruit of the true Vine.

Since no fermented substance was allowed on the altar,[73] only nonalcoholic wine might be used for drink offerings. The Hebrews could have used several methods to produce this. Raisins steeped in water until soft and then squeezed to produce the elixir was one way. Freshly expressed grape juice slowly heated until evaporated to half to one third of its volume,[74] and later reconstituted by the addition of water was another.[75] Did this mingled water and "wine" look ahead to the twin streams which flowed from the pierced heart of Jesus?[76]

Ellen White has left us this perceptive insight: "The Bible nowhere teaches the use of intoxicating wine, either as a beverage or as a symbol of the blood of Christ. We appeal to the natural reason whether the blood of Christ is better represented by the pure juice of the grape in its natural state, or after it has been converted into fermented and intoxicating wine. We maintain that the former is the only symbol properly representing the sacred blood of Christ, and a symbol established by himself; and we urge that the latter should never be placed upon the Lord's table."[77] What is right for the Lord's table is also right for the Lord's ancient altar.

Scripture uses libations as illustrations of the dedication of life's energy. While Jacob was trying to escape from Laban the Lord "appeared . . . and blessed him. And God said . . . , Thy name shall not be called any more Jacob, but Israel."[78] Jehovah then repeated the terms of the covenants[79] He had made with Abraham[80] and Isaac[81] and invited Jacob to accept them. To signal his compliance, "Jacob set up a pillar in the place where he talked with him, . . . and he poured[82] a drink offering thereon, and he poured[83] oil thereon."[84] This is the very first libation mentioned in Scripture and represents Jacob's will poured out in surrender to the covenant, while the oil typifies the endorsing Spirit.

Harried by Saul, David sighed for a drink from the spring of Bethlehem. Risking their lives, three of his companions passed through enemy lines and filled a pitcher for their beloved leader. On being presented with it, David exclaimed in awe, "My God forbid it me, that I should do this thing." Therefore he "poured[85] it out to the Lord."[86] David's libation of water from the spring of Bethlehem commemorated the lives risked to bless him and whispered of the water of life which poured from the pierced heart of the Man of Bethlehem.

The apostle referred to this ceremony in his last letter to Timothy. Condemned to death and sensing the executioner's sword glinting down his path, Paul wrote: "I am already being poured out as a drink offering."[87] The form of his verb[88] pictures his voluntary share in his act. The Old Testament verb [89] also calls attention to the participation of the worshiper. For three decades Paul had daily laid himself upon the altar of service,[90] and its flames had seared his body. Now the time had come for him to pour out his blood as a libation as the consummation of his dedication. Remembering Israel's ancient rite, Paul knew that the devotee had provided his own libation. In his mind's eye he could see the priest pouring the wine upon the sacrifice being consumed on the altar, and in his cell he sensed that he must be ready at any moment to give his own blood.

He had expressed his readiness for this to his Philippian friends, reminding them that he was eager to pour his blood as a libation upon[91] the sacrificial testimony of their lives.[92] Writing to Timothy he added that the time for this was close at hand. The word he used to describe his "departure"[93] pictures the loosing of a ship from her moorings. Paul could hear the slap of the tide on her hull and feel her tugging impatiently at anchor, eager to sail out to her final haven. In this context he showed the meaning of the drink offering to be the filling up, or bringing to their consummation, of "the afflictions of Christ."[94]

God Himself twice used the drink offering as an illustration of His Son's fulfillment of the sacrificial demands of the divine government. He revealed that from the beginning, "Wisdom," the personification of Him who had planned and carried out the creation of the universe, had been "poured out"[95] as a libation over the eternal throne.[96] This distillation of Christ's character and work, His power and love, is thus represented as pervading the governance of heaven. Seeing this, all created beings constantly adore Him as Creator by singing "the old song."[97]

God prophetically exposed the hostility which His Son was to suffer at the hands of His own, Herod, and the Roman soldiers,[98] which culminated in His crucifixion. This apparent tragedy, however, would be followed by His resurrection and ascension in triumph. The psalmist then depicted the rejoicing Father as "pouring out"[99] the redemptive essence of His Son as a libation over His throne on the "mount of His sanctuary."[100] At Jesus' inauguration as Sacrifice and Priest, the Father granted His Son the heathen as His inheritance.[101] Henceforth the ransomed hosts will adore Him as the Redeemer by singing "the new song."[102]

By saturating His throne with the libation of His Son's redemptive essence, the Father called upon the universe to realize that all that His throne, this symbol of Divine rulership, had eternally represented was now immeasurably enriched and glorified by the addition of the life-essence of the victorious Creator-Redeemer and Victim-Priest. John viewed the bleeding Lamb in the very act of pouring out His blood on the throne.[103] As the consummation of His completed sacrifice [104] the libation of Christ's triumphant blood bathed the throne of the Eternal with the added radiance of redemptive love. In appreciation our hearts should cry out, "Lord, I can do no less than lay all I *am* and *have* as willing gifts upon Thy altar!"

Chapter 3

The Peace Offering

All my *joy* is Christ's

The peace offering, one of Israel's most joyous celebrations, might be presented at any time by individuals or the community. The sacred meal which concluded the ritual high-lighted fellowship with God, the worshiper's Host, as well as Guest. Its Hebrew name *shelem*, derived from *shalom*, suggests fulfillment, since peace offerings followed sin and burnt offerings to complete the sacrificial cycle. Signifying wholeness and restitution, shalom describes peace with an enemy,[1] harmony between allies,[2] and the results of the covenant with God.[3]

The peace offering expressed joy at difficulties resolved, pledges paid, business completed, and accord with Heaven through faith and submission.[4] The Hebrew for peace offering is always in the plural and suggests peace of many kinds—mental, physical, social, and spiritual. Four times the Lord declared that the law regulating this celebration was a "perpetual statute."[5] The ideas of completeness, soundness, health, peace, prosperity, and tranquility cluster around *shalom* and this ritual like a halo.

The peace offering was the only sacrifice climaxed by a fellowship banquet in which God, the priest, and the worshiper joined. It has appropriately been explained as "a shared-offering."[6] Man actually owns nothing; God is the Possessor of "the cattle upon a thousand hills."[7] After providing His people with everything, He asked them to return a gift to His sanctuary, later handing back to His faithful ones the makings of a feast of joy. The worshipers acknowledged His goodness and responded to His invitation, "Open the door, I will come in to him, and will sup with him, and he with me."[8] The peace offering and its eucharistic meal expressed their devotion and hope for the kingdom of the Messiah.[9]

The formula "sacrifice of peace offerings" called attention to the slaughter which was the basis of this rite. "Peace sacrifice" might be a more vivid translation. In fact, inspiration used "sacrifice"[10] by itself almost one hundred times to designate the ritual meal which accompanied this rite.[11] Focusing on the victim's death, this word looks forward to the crucifixion, without which there could be no peace.

The Lord recommended that every animal used for food should be butchered at the sanctuary and its blood splashed on the altar.[12] This rule was modified in the Promised Land for those who lived too far from the tabernacle.[13] The rabbis understood that God required a specific technique for this slaughter,[14] and even today the Semitic world invokes the name of Deity when butchering any animal. This kept before the Israelites that death resulted from sin, and reminded them that the victim laid down its life to sustain them in the name of the Lord. This act anticipated the Saviour's dying at the Father's mandate to provide "meat" and "drink" for all. As Christians, we should never forget that the "cross of Calvary is stamped on every loaf" of bread.[15]

The term *sacrifice* also evoked ideas of a blood covenant. By eating the victim's flesh, the participants were fused into an organic whole.[16] Christ embodied these concepts in the communion service. This new-covenant meal has kept before His disciples the idea that they are members of His "body." The "flesh" and "blood" of the Incarnate Word represents His life of perfect obedience and His will of absolute submission,[17] qualities revealed in the inspired Word.[18] By reading, believing, and practicing its principles, Christians grow in grace to become like their Master.

Any Israelite might choose from among the creatures permitted,[19] and present his sacrifice whenever he wished. The priest examined the animal and accompanied the worshiper to the place of slaughter, where he bound and threw it. In burnt and sin offerings the penitent confessed, but Maimonedes remembered that in peace offerings he laid his hands on his substitute's head and enumerated the blessings he had received, before slashing its throat.[20] The priest caught its blood in a bowl and carried it to the altar to splash its four sides.[21] This "sprinkled blood" made the atonement. The Talmud declared,

"Whenever the blood touches the altar the offerer is atoned for."[22] This "gift" of blood represented the "life" of the substitute presented to God on behalf of the sinner. The priest poured the remainder at the base of the altar.

The offerer proceeded to skin and "rightly divide" the carcass, allowing the priest to take its hide and "breast" as his perquisites.[23] Originally considered as belonging to God,[24] the breast was presented to Him by the priest in his act of heaving it up before the altar.[25] The Lord then gave it back, shown by bringing it down[26] and "waving" it from side to side before the Lord to acknowledge His sovereignty.[27]

The "inwards" and fat or suet, and in the case of sheep, the fat tail, were washed and salted. The caul, a part of the liver, and the two kidneys were surrendered to the Lord as His special "food" or "bread."[28] When placed on the altar, called "the table of the Lord,"[29] they were consumed upon the burnt offering already smoldering there.[30] The sacred fire was the symbol of God's accepting presence.[31]

These "inwards" represent the secret and precious part of the victim and point forward to the inner dynamics and drives of the Substitute so much appreciated by the Father, who found His "reins and heart" a treasure of the greatest value. Until these had been consumed, the ritual meal could not be eaten. For us all, every Christian joy rests on the foundation of Calvary.

The priest's portions were the "breast" and "right shoulder." Breast reminds us of the comfort and nourishment provided by a mother, while shoulder suggests the strength and support given by a father. The rejoicing Shepherd lifts His rescued sheep above danger, saying, in effect, "He shall dwell between [My] shoulders,"[32] and thus He answers the prayer, "Set me as a seal upon thine heart, as a seal upon thy arm."[33]

Jehovah regarded the smoke ascending from the peace offering as a "sweet savor"[34] and expressed His satisfaction with the worshiper by completely vaporizing His share of the covenant banquet.

Peace offerings were always to be accompanied with appropriate meal and drink offerings.[35] These unleavened cakes, wafers, or fried pieces were "eaten" by all three parties, God, the priest, and the people. They formed the concluding part of the festivities,[36] and were calculated in strict proportion to the kind of victim sacrificed.[37] Should the worshiper choose, he might even bring "leavened bread" for certain kinds of peace offerings, but no part of this was ever placed on the altar.

Although the larger part of the sacrifice would be the worshiper's, the whole was presented to God, who was thus served first. He then returned their shares to His ministering priest and adoring people. Jesus followed this principle in the upper room by offering Himself to God as our Sacrifice. The Father then gave His Son to His followers, who accepted His invitation to eat His flesh and drink His blood.[38]

The offerer cooked his portions in any manner he chose so long as it was "in a holy place." This was originally understood to mean within the court of the tabernacle, but was later interpreted by the rabbis to include any location within the walls of the Holy City. While the celebrant generally invited his family and friends to join him,[39] Jesus recommended that the poor, blind, and crippled should not be forgotten.[40] Moses had long before warned against excluding the Levites.[41] Meanwhile the priest and his family prepared their portions,[42] and feasted in the joy of service.[43]

All participants must be ceremonially clean or risk being "cut off."[44] This anticipated the purity of the bride at the "marriage supper of the Lamb" when clothed in the wedding garment of her Bridegroom's righteousness.

The law recommended peace offerings for three situations in the lives of the worshiper:[45] (i) to praise God's name, extol His character, and glorify His goodness and mercy; (ii) to express thankfulness for some specific blessing; and (iii) to celebrate the completion of a vow not to do something in His honor, or a promise to carry out some project.

Peace offerings of praise and adoration must be eaten the day they were presented[46] to display the eagerness of the participants. These eucharistic banquets were occasions for the worshipers to share their feelings about God,[47] and, as they drank "the cup of salvation," they "offered the sacrifice of thanksgiving"[48] to their Creator.[49]

Paul called upon Christians to "offer the sacrifice of praise to God continually"[50] in appreciation of Christ's death, and then to communicate their joy to others. But even these services might degenerate into occasions of ostentation.[51] "Oh that men would praise the Lord for his goodness, and for his wonderful works to the children of men! And let them sacrifice the sacrifices of thanksgiving, and declare his works with rejoicing," or singing.[52]

The peace offering expressed gratitude for specific benefits received, particularly forgiveness of sin.[53] To encourage Moses and Israel to leave the conflicts of Egypt, Jehovah promised that they would assuredly offer peace offerings in the Promised Land,[54] with "every man under his vine and under his fig tree."

In the New Testament the influence of *shalom* is seen in the Greek *eirene*. Messianic peace, resulting from the death of the Lamb of God,[55] lies at the foundation of Christian joy. The paradoxical prediction, "the chastisement of our peace is upon him" should be understood in this context. Because He suffered, His disciples enjoy life. The "gospel of peace"[56] flows from the Christian's heart as he realizes that he is the purchase of His death. Because a new covenant relationship now exists between God and man, resulting from the atonement,[57] untroubled well-being results. Paul's grasp of this relationship caused him to invoke Heaven's peace upon all the communities to whom he wrote his epistles.[58]

The Lord designed the peace offering so that the participants might experience the "peace of God."[59] Conscious reconciliation with Heaven results in this enjoyment. At such celebrations God accepted any offering, even defective ones,[60] and even with leavened bread,[61] so long as the worshipers were sincere and enthusiastic.[62]

The third reason for presenting a peace offering was the fulfillment of a vow.[63] This must be ratified at the sanctuary and not at home. There the whole family joined the priest in the celebrations and the worship of Jehovah.[64]

The rabbis differentiate between a vow and an oath. The vow, they suggest, was a decision not to do something,[65] while an oath was a resolution to carry out some project for the glory of God.[66] But in either case the Lord warned that it was better not to vow than to fail to carry it out.[67] He praised any one who "sweareth to his own hurt, and changeth not."[68] Ananias and Sapphira promised to do something for the cause of God, and then reneged,[69] with terrible consequences. The Nazarite who vowed not to drink wine or cut his hair for a specified period presented a peace offering to celebrate the completion of his resolve.[70] Paul was persuaded to join some brethren in offering such a sacrifice at the conclusion of a temporary Nazarite vow.[71]

The earliest peace offering to bind a covenant is found in the story of Jacob and Laban. A cairn of rocks was erected as a boundary marker on the very spot where Jacob had vowed to serve God twenty years earlier.[72] The parties promised not to molest each other, and Jacob then slew a peace offering, calling upon the Lord to ratify the agreement. The feast which followed endorsed the "covenant of salt," and the next morning the families returned to their respective homes.

Asaph predicted that the Messiah would gather His saints into a happy band of celebrants at His second coming, because these victors had long before covenanted to serve God through peace offerings.[73] For Christians his meaning is clear. The sacrifice of Calvary alone can ratify the new covenant with heaven. This truth is reiterated in every Communion service.

When Christ was about to die as the Peace Offering,[74] He bequeathed His peace to His church.[75] As He stood in the shadow of Gethsemane He fulfilled the psalmist's promise to the obedient: "Great peace have they which love thy law, and nothing shall offend them."[76] The apostle affirmed that "peace with God through our Lord Jesus Christ"[77] might be enjoyed by all who were "sometime alienated and enemies," but whom Jesus "reconciled in the body of his flesh through death."[78] Our Lord's postresurrection greeting, "Peace!" attests to the fact that His death had ratified the everlasting covenant of grace. He thus fulfilled the promise of the angels at His birth, "Peace on earth!" And when He returns in triumph for His blood-bought covenant people, it will be as "the Prince of peace."

Through Christ's sacrifice there flows into warring humanity the river of peace, for only in His perfect obedience is there perfect peace, and the realization of the promise.[79] As we feed on Jesus as our Peace Offering in the eucharistic banquet He has provided, we enter into the joy and fulfillment which flow from His life. Day by day we have peace in the gospel because all our *joy* is in Christ.

Chapter 4

The Sin Offering

All my *sins* are Christ's

Inspiration defines sin as aggression against God's law[1] or falling short of its standards[2] through lack of faith[3] stemming from a refusal to do the right we know.[4] There is no accounting for sin, because it has no reason for being. Prior to Creation sin strutted before the Eternal's throne and defied His authority. Sin led to war and caused the expulsion of unnumbered angels from the bliss of heaven. Sin slithered into Eden's scented bowers and, with silken words and specious promises, stripped the robe of light from mankind and plunged this world into darkness and death.[5]

To cure the deadly malady produced by the fruit of rebellion's tree, God introduced a Physician with a precious antidote, and promised that all who chose His treatment would be healed. But to accomplish this, the Physician Himself would need to die in the sinner's place and provide the cleansing with His blood. And to symbolize this substitutionary death, the sacrificial system was revealed to Adam and Eve at Eden's gate, and by them passed on to their descendants.[6]

At Sinai God again taught the details of the plan of salvation, compacted in the sanctuary and its furnishing and displayed through its systems of the priesthood, the sacrifices, and the ceremonial feasts. To illustrate the Saviour's agony and His vicarious death, the Lord designed the sin offering to deal with sins committed in ignorance, as well as knowingly.[7]

We like to think that ignorance excuses guilt, or at least renders the sinner deserving of mercy, and we sometimes equate ignorance with innocence. Because "the natural man" loves "darkness rather than light,"[8] some prefer to remain ignorant, hoping to escape responsibility for their conduct. But the slaughter of the sin offering for sins of ignorance displays God's answer to this rationalization. The Lord called the inadvertent infractions of His expressed will "sins" and imposed death on the substitute to underline the culpability of their perpetrators. On the cross Jesus the Priest prayed for forgiveness for those who were unaware of the crime they were committing, and then Jesus the victim died in their places.[9] Stephen understood that the injustices against him were done in ignorance, yet needed Divine pardon.[10] Saul of Tarsus, who helped to lynch him, acknowledged himself the chief of sinners when convicted by the Spirit of his heinous act.[11]

Inspiration uses one Hebrew word, *chatta'th*, and one Greek word, *harmatria*, for both "sin" and "sin offering." English translators overlook this, but the careful reader should be alert to this revealing usage. When the penitent brought his sin offering to the sanctuary, he brought his sin. The Lord assured Cain that should he sin, his "sin offering"[12] was crouching nearby, ready to spring into action on his behalf. Paul wrote that God had "made" Jesus to be a sin offering for all mankind, although He "knew no sin" personally.[13] While *chatta'th* means "to miss the goal"[14]or target",[15] or "to slip off a path,"[16] its intensive or piel form emphasizes the results of the sin offering, i.e. making reconciliation or atonement,[17] cleansing,[18] purging or purifying.[19] David used this idiom with great perspicacity in his prayer-poem: "Purge me [sin offering me] with hyssop, and I shall be clean."[20]

Several details of the sin offering were similar to those of burnt and peace offerings. The penitent found a suitable bull calf,[21] which God had provided in the first place,[22] and presented it as his substitute. He bound and threw it in the designated place, and, laying both hands on its head, silently confessed his specific sin,[23] symbolically transferring his guilt to the creature.[24] Taking a knife, he slit its throat, while the priest caught its blood in a golden bowl.

The priest administered the blood in one of two ways, depending upon the category of the worshiper. In the first ceremony, the four steps took place in both the holy place and the court. The ministrant carried the blood into the sanctuary, and, standing between the golden altar and the innermost veil, sprinkled some of it seven times before and on this tapestry.[25] Seven underlined the completeness of the sprinkling.[26] Moving to the front of the altar of incense, he smeared its four horns[27] by dipping his finger into the blood once for each, thus making atonement for the sinner. Although he could not actually see the priest, the penitent accepted this mediation on his behalf by faith.[28]

These actions anticipated Christ's work on His entry into the celestial holy place with His own blood.[29] There must first be a "spilling" of the blood in the court for there to be a "sprinkling" in the holy place to complete the transaction and make atonement. Returning to the court, the priest poured the residue of the blood at the foot of the altar of burnt offering to form the foundation of its ministry.[30] The unique part of this rite was the priest's use of the blood to record the confessed and forgiven sins of the penitent on the veil and the four horns of the altar of incense.

In the second ceremony, the blood was ministered in two stages, both in the court. Mounting the ramp to the platform around the altar of perpetual sacrifice, the priest smeared the blood on its four horns with his finger and poured what was left at its base.[31] In both rites the priest's bloody fingerprints left mute records of confessed sins on the horns of both altars. These remained throughout the year, until "cleansed" by the ceremonies of the Day of Atonement.

The carcasses were also treated in two ways. The body of the victim, whose blood had been brought into the holy place, together with its skin, viscera, and dung,[32] was burned "without the camp."[33] At the same time its suet, or the fat from its insides, was vaporized on the altar.[34] Paul perceived that this illustrated the purpose and place of the crucifixion: "Wherefore Jesus also, that he might sanctify the people [nations] with his own blood, suffered without the gate."[35]

The carcass whose blood was sprinkled on the horns of the brazen altar was treated like a peace offering. Skinned and dissected by the penitent, washed and salted, its suet burned by the priest, its body was then given to the ministrant to be eaten[36] in a place designated "holy." Unlike peace offerings, the members of the priest's family were not permitted to partake. When the number of sin offerings made this an impossibility, a morsel as large as an olive sufficed.[37] This was in keeping with the biblical principle which permitted a part to represent the whole.[38] Eating symbolized the priest's identification with the victim, and so with the sinner, and typified Jesus, both the Victim and the Priest.

Some question whether blood was splattered *on* the veil. Five pieces of evidence have convinced this investigator that it indeed was. (i) The Hebrew preposition rendered "before"[39] takes the accusative case as its direct object when it follows a verb of motion, and then literally means "to, in, or on" the face or front of the veil. This prepositional expression is different from that rendered "before [the face of] the Lord,"[40] which is in the locative case. The same term is translated "upon" in this sentence: "He burnt incense upon the altar." [41] (ii) The Septuagint uses the word *kata*, meaning "down on" when used with the accusative, as in this case. (iii) The Mishnah remembers that in sin offerings burned outside the camp, "the blood required to be sprinkled upon the veil and upon the golden altar." [42] Another tractate notes: "The seven sprinklings between the [carrying] bars [where the priest stood before the ark on the Day of atonement] and those on the veil [of the holy of holies] and those on the golden altar."[43] (iv) The Talmud contains an eye-witness description of the veil which Titus took as a trophy of his destruction of Jerusalem and pillage of its temple in A.D. 70: "I saw it in Rome, and there were upon it many drops of blood both of the bullock and the he-goat of the Day of Atonement." [44] (v) This veil was changed annually, probably because it was splashed with blood. Ellen White remembered that "at the moment in which Christ died . . . the vail of the temple, a strong, rich drapery *that had been renewed yearly*, was rent in twain." [45]

Type and prophecy should have indicated to Israel that all their *sins* are Christ's and that one day the judgment would convene, and the record books be opened so that their evidence might be considered. The result for all whose confessed and forgiven sins have gone before unto judgment will be a decision of vindication and acquittal. This ritual we shall consider in the following chapter.

Chapter 5
The Day of Atonement

All my *guilt* is Christ's

The morning and evening sacrifices continued in the sanctuary every day, including sabbaths and festivals. In addition, "day by day the repentant sinner brought his offering to the door of the tabernacle and, placing his hand upon the victim's head, confessed his sins, thus in figure transferring them from himself to the innocent sacrifice. The animal was then slain. . . . The blood, representing the forfeited life of the sinner, whose guilt the victim bore, was carried by the priest into the holy place and sprinkled before the veil, behind which was the ark containing the law that the sinner had transgressed. By this ceremony the sin was, through the blood, transferred in figure to the sanctuary. In some cases the blood was not taken into the holy place; but the flesh was then to be eaten by the priest. . . . Both ceremonies alike symbolized the transfer of the sin from the penitent to the sanctuary."[1]

The Lord designed that these crimson records should remain as mute testimony of confessed and forgiven sin, which ceremonially defiled the sanctuary and needed eventual cleansing and removal. This was done on the Day of Atonement, which fell on the tenth day of Tishri, Israel's seventh month,[2] a day which provided for the "annual reminder of [those] sins,"[3] as well as ceremonies for their eradication. These rites cleansed[4] the sanctuary and God's people, while nonparticipants were "cut off." [5]

On the first day of Tishri, the *shofar* or ram's horn alerted Israel to the approaching crisis when the Judge, having scrutinized each case as a shepherd examines his sheep, would pass sentence on the tenth.[6] During these "ten days of penitence" "many pious Jews prepared themselves for these moving ceremonies by fasting, praying (cf. Lev 23:27; Num 29:7, 'like the feasts,' Moed Katan 3:6), and ritual ablutions, and even making a retreat. The high priest . . . was obliged . . . to sanctify himself by prayer. The Day of Atonement, Yom Kippur, was so important that if a man spoke simply of 'the day' [cf. Heb 20:25], everyone knew that he meant this particular day."[7] Rabbi Isaac Hershon remembered the old Jewish belief, and explained that "the Day of Atonement was the day of judgment."[8]

The Lord required Yom Kippur to be observed as a "sabbath of rest"[9] and urged every worshiper to "afflict his soul"[10] by disciplining his appetites.[11] This fast, the only one prescribed in the law, alluded to by Jeremiah as "the fasting day"[12] and emphasized by Isaiah,[13] focuses attention on "the last days" and the final day of judgment.[14] Paul sensed the eschatological overtones of this ritual, and urged his Hebrew Christian readers to prepare themselves with increased urgency as they saw "the day" approaching.[15] The precise dating of Yom Kippur by the law prepared students of prophecy for the equally precise announcement, "The hour of his judgment is come."[16] This moment occurred at the antitypical day of atonement at the end of the 2300th prophetic "evening morning" sanctuary-cleansing ceremony.[17] An understanding of this ancient ritual will clarify what is currently transpiring and explain the ministry of our High Priest in His celestial tabernacle.

The high priest performed all the ceremonies of the Day of Atonement, including the morning and evening sacrifices,[18] and, if the day fell on the Sabbath, the extra Sabbath services as well. These regular priestly ministries, like familiar arms embracing the unique rites of the Day, taught the worshiper that Jesus the Priest constantly grants forgiveness and ever lives to pour grace and mercy on all who turn to Him.[19] The Scriptures provide some details of the Day's activities, and the following scenario is devised with the help of additional Jewish records.

After completing the morning service the high priest laid aside his "golden robes" and put on the clothes of an ordinary priest,[20] to signal the surrender of his honored position and his assumption of the role of a servant. His act depicted the "self-emptying"[21] of our Intercessor, who laid "aside his royal robe and kingly crown, [and] clothed his divinity with humanity,"[22] and "taking the form of a servant . . . offered sacrifice, Himself the priest, Himself the victim."[23] Israel's high priest wore his "golden garments" for all the "daily" services which he performed during the Day, and changed into the uniform of an ordinary priest only for the unique rites of the Day of Atonement.

The high priest conducted two rituals to establish his personal right to act as the representative of God's people for the special rites of the Day. He presented a bull as a sin offering "for himself, and, for his house,"[24] for which he paid with his own resources,[25] as Christ did in giving Himself. Laying his hands on its head he made confession, and then moved to a small receptical called Calpi.[26] This contained two identical lots, which some remember were of boxwood, while others aver were of gold.[27] Plunging his hands into the urn, he took one out in each, and, striding toward the goats tethered in the court, placed a fist on the head of each. The Israelites considered it propitious should the lot for the Lord's goat appear in his right hand. This is the first use of lots in Scripture. After Divine selection had rendered the results valid,[28] a "thread of crimson wool" was tied around the throat of the Lord's goat to mark him for slaughter, while another was bound about the horns of Azazel's animal[29] to display that his power had been contained by this crimson symbol of death. Azazel's goat was then turned to face the people, while the Lord's looked toward His oracle. The perceptive worshipers sensed that one day the Antitype would be set apart to die "by the determinate counsel and foreknowledge of God."[30]

Returning to his bull, the high priest repeated his confession,[31] and, slaughtering it, caught its blood in a golden bowl, which he handed to an assistant to stir lest it coagulate[32] while he performed the first rite for his personal validation.

Filling a golden censer with embers from the altar of burnt offering, and a golden ladle with two handfuls of incense,[33] the high priest passed through the holy place[34] with the fire pan in his right hand and the perfume in his left. Reaching the northern edge of the innermost veil, he drew it aside with his left elbow and stepped into God's golden shrine, allowing the tapestry to drop into place behind him. Keeping his eyes on the ark in utmost respect, he sidled southward until his left foot touched the golden rod used for carrying the ark. Stepping over this, He remained between the rods as he moved toward the mercy seat. Placing the censer on the floor before the ark,[35] he poured the incense over the coals, and the oracle was flooded with fragrance. The apostle evidently had this ceremony in mind in his letter to the Hebrews,[36] since the Day of Atonement was the only occasion on which the most holy place contained the censer, interpretively explained as "altar" in some modern paraphrases.

The high priest then backed until he touched the veil. Keeping his gaze on the Shekinah, he sidled southward, and stepping over the other carrying rod, continued to the wall. Lifting the curtain with his right elbow, he backed out of the most holy place, allowing the drapery to fall into place. The rabbis remember that he paused to pray for Israel, but opined that he should not prolong his intercession lest his delay cause anxiety to the people.[37] His brief intercession ended, he turned and walked into the court.

This initial entry by Israel's high priest into God's presence with incense, symbol of "the merits and intercession of Christ,"[38] foreshadowed the opening act in the high priestly ministry of the Saviour. Jesus laid the foundation of His mediation in prayer,[39] displaying His concern for "his own" and was "heard" by His Father for His "strong crying and tears."[40] Like Aaron, He interceded for Himself as well as " 'his house'—that is, his wife."[41] The church in all ages is Christ's bride;[42] for her He died, and for her He intercedes.

Back in the court the High priest carried out his second act of validation. Taking the container of bull's blood, he retraced his steps until he stood a second time before the Shekinah, now enveloped by the cloud of fragrance irradiated with "the rainbow encircling the throne [representing] the combined power of mercy and justice"[43] and redolent with the sweetness of accepted intercession. Dipping his finger into the bowl he sprinkled the blood "as though he were wielding a whip,"[44] once upon the mercy seat and seven times on the ground where the censer burned.[45] The "sprinkled" blood now symbolically reigned "in the midst of the throne."[46] He then left the oracle, as he had previously, and, setting the bull's blood on "the golden stand" near the altar of incense, went out to the court.[47]

The high priest's return from his second encounter with the Being gloriously enthroned in the most holy place assured the worshipers that he had been accepted as their mediator and was now empowered to conduct the unique ritual of the Day connected with the two goats. Each of the high priest's acts illustrated some aspect of Christ's ministry, and these two entries into the oracle were not exceptions. Some question whether Jesus needed to present His own sin offering in the celestial tabernacle for God's approval, since He had already been endorsed by both the Father and the Spirit at His baptism,[48] twice by the inspired baptizer at Jordan,[49] and once by His Father just prior to Calvary.[50] Of course, the Saviour did not *need* any validation! But let us see how the Father gave it to Him in His own way and for His own purpose.

On the morning of the resurrection the Saviour delayed His return to heaven long enough to comfort a weeping woman. To Mary's act of adoration He gently remonstrated, "Touch me not; for I am not yet ascended to my Father."[51] This was in accordance with the law, for while he was ministering, the high priest was forbidden to touch anyone or anything lest he become defiled. "Jesus refused to receive the homage of his people until he knew that his sacrifice [blood] had been accepted by the Father. . . . He also had a request to prefer [incense] concerning his chosen ones. . . . His church must be justified and accepted before he could accept heavenly honor. . . . God's answer to this appeal goes forth in the proclamation: 'Let all the angels of God worship him.' "[52]

The "type which Christ fulfilled in connection with His first ascension was that of the high priest presenting the [bull's] blood in the holy of holies on the Day of Atonement. Thus Christ the true High Priest ministered His own blood, and acceptance of that sacrifice for sins answers every need of the sinner forever."[53] God's endorsement of Israel's high priest on his two entries into the most holy place, with incense and blood, pointed to Christ's ratification by His Father as both Intercessor and Sacrifice at His first ascension on the morning of the resurrection. The authorized high priest's two acts thus far were preparatory to his performance of the unique service of the Day.

Continuing now: As the opening act of the special Day of Atonement services, the high priest slew Yahweh's goat as Israel's sin offering and caught its blood in a golden bowl. Moving into the oracle for the third time, he did with the goat's blood as he had done with the bull's. Back in the holy place, he put the container of the goat's blood "on the second stand in the sanctuary" and took the bull's blood from its stand. Dipping his finger into it, he sprinkled once upward, and seven times downward before the veil, dipping each time, so that the blood splattered "upon the veil."[54] Returning the bull's blood to its stand, he did with the goat's blood as he had done with the bull's. Then, emptying the remainder of the bull's blood into the goat's blood, he poured the mixture into the container of the bull's blood. This careful mingling of the blood of both animals displayed the truth that the two sacrifices were one and the same, for Christ is not divisible. Smearing some on the four horns of the golden altar in an anticlockwise direction starting from the northwest horn,[55] he moved the censer, used in the morning service, from its place in the center of the top of the golden altar, smeared blood "seven times" on this spot, and then replaced the censer in the center. These blood rites displayed the truths that the blood of the one great Sacrifice lay at the center of intercession, and that it was this "sprinkled" blood which made atonement for the holy place.

Moving back to the court, the high priest made atonement for the brazen altar by smearing blood on its four horns and "seven times" sprinkling its four sides.[56] The residue of the mingled blood he poured at the altar's southern base.[57]

The high priest had now reached a very important point in the proceedings of the Day. The Scriptures declare that he had made "an end of reconciling the holy place, and the tabernacle . . . and the altar" [58] and had completed the "cleansing" of the sanctuary from the "uncleanness of the children of Israel," that is, from "the sins of the entire Jewish people, accumulated during the year just ended . . . in the sanctuary."[59]

These ceremonies taught that the blood of the goat provided a complete cover-up for the records of all confessed sins. Wycliffe dynamically translated this Hebrew word meaning "cover"[60] as "at-one-ment." Through this ritual the Israelites were to look forward to the Day of Atonement in the celestial sanctuary, also called the day of judgment, during which the divine High Priest will apply the merits of His atoning death by "sprinkling" His blood, which had previously been "spilled" on Calvary, to cover up the records of the confessed sins of all His people in every age, which have gone before unto judgment[61] through repentance. Those who accept this ministry will be declared "cleansed," and their names will be retained in God's ledger of the living, while all others will be "cut off," [62] and their names blotted out.

In explaining these effects, Moses introduced words that anticipate this meaning. He stressed no fewer than sixteen times[63] that the blood "covers up" the recorded sins, thus making atonement for the sanctuary and the people. The result of this cover-up was a threefold cleansing,[64] once for the altar and twice for the people.[65] Only those whose sins had been previously "covered" by the daily sin offering were now declared "cleansed." This term *taher* describes one who is ritually and morally clean. Because his confessed, forgiven, and forsaken sins had "gone before unto judgment" and were recorded as such in the sanctuary by the sprinkled blood, the worshiper was declared clean.

Job's question, phrased in Hebrew poetic form,[66] places "cleanse" (*taher*) as the equivalent of the word to "make righteous" (*zadaq*).[67] The effect of the first is to bring about the second. Rabbi Kalisch remarked, "After the atonement of the high priest, and of the people the holy edifice itself remained to be expiated, for both the structure and all its parts, and the sacred utensils and implements were deemed to have been defiled by the transgressions of the Israelites through the year."[68] This task completed, the entire sanctuary was restored to its pristine state of cleanliness. Israel's rituals were enacted parables of the ministry of the Messiah, and were so understood. Rabbi Akiba reminded his people that their attention should be focused on a celestial transaction: "Blessed are ye, O Israel. Before whom are ye made clean and who makes you clean? Your Father in heaven."[69]

After completing his "cleansing" and "hallowing" of the sanctuary, and his making the people "clean from all [their] sins," the high priest stood in a position of great authority. He had paid the ransom price in the blood of the Lord's goat for the sins of Israel and held them, as it were, in his personal possession. His next task was to dispose of them in God's appointed way. Striding up to Azazel's goat, he laid his hands on his head, and by confession, placed them all upon the goat.

This mysterious rite is a unique Day of Atonement ritual. When the goats had been selected by Divine lot, one was designated "for Yahweh" and the other "for Azazel." Since Yahweh is a personal name for the Deity, many Bible students consider that Azazel must also be a personal name, but for a being who stands in opposition to God. Others have suggested that Azazel may mean "sending away," while still others propose that it may refer to a locality. Gesenius perceptively observed that neither an action, nor a region can ever form a natural contrast with Yahweh; only a person can. Azazel must, therefore, be the name of a character whose life and purpose are the opposite of God's.

Further, the preposition *for*,[70] used with both goats, must be given the same force in each case. If it describes a relationship with the person called Yahweh, it must also indicate a similar relationship with the person called Azazel. The Lord's goat represented the Lord. Azazel's goat must represent Azazel. Almost a century ago Carl Frederich Keil affirmed, "The view that Azazel is the designation of an evil spirit dwelling in the wilderness (Spencer, Rosenmuler, Gesenius) is now almost universally acknowledged."[71] No valid evidence has appeared during the intervening years to cast a doubt on this conclusion.

Another reason to identify Azazel with the devil was the defilement which his goat caused to the one who conducted him into the wilderness.[72] Sin offerings did not defile, they cleansed.[73] Azazel's goat, laden with Israel's guilt, could not therefore be a sin offering, for without the shedding of its blood it could bring about no remission of sin. Azazel's goat played a role only after Israel's guilt had been removed from the people.

The punctuation of the King James Version has occasionally given rise to the notion that Azazel's goat performed a part in this "atonement."[74] But may I translate this passage literally? It seems clear that it is written in the form of a chiasmus.

Lord's goat (dead) — Aaron shall cause-to-be-brought-near the goat upon which came the lot for Yahweh, and he shall-make-it-to-be-a-sin-offering.

Azazel's goat (alive) — But the goat on which came the lot for Azazel, he shall-make-to-stand-alive before the face of Yahweh.

Lord's goat (dead) — So as to [LXX] make-atonement with him;

Azazel's goat (alive) — and to let him go for Azazel into the wilderness.

Since atonement requires blood, and Azazel's goat supplied no blood, no atonement can be made through him. The rites connected with Azazel's goat point to occurrences in the experience of the devil, as we shall see.

God first faced sin on this planet in Eden. There He held an investigative judgment on the cases of Adam, Eve, and the serpent, although He was already aware of every detail of what had transpired. He then passed judgment on the serpent, Eve, and Adam in the reverse order of their trials, sentencing the serpent first because he was the most guilty. The Divine decree exposed the serpent's responsibility in the guilt of every person whom he had seduced.

It seems clear that there are two parts of every sin: Satan's temptation and the sinner's act. In God's final dealing with the cases of His saints, Satan's role will not be ignored. This truth is the basis for this Day of Atonement ceremony. Azazel's goat symbolically bore the devil's responsibility for Israel's sins. Loaded with this guilt by the high priest, Satan's goat, representing Satan himself, was led away into a land not inhabited, and there released.

The Hebrew phrase "into the wilderness" designates a location apparently well known to Israel and throws light on the request of the exorcised demons not to be sent by Christ into "the deep" before their time.[75] These devils "believed"[76] in their inescapable destination! "The demonic identification [of Azazel] would indicate that the original purpose of the ritual was to get rid of the evil by banishing it into its original source."[77] Driven into an "uninhabited" land, Azazel's goat was left to wander as a spectacle to all.

The eschatology of this rite seems clear. Following the conclusion of the services of the antitypical day of atonement in the celestial sanctuary, our High Priest will return to this earth to bless His people. Then the righteous will be taken to heaven to be with their Lord, while the wicked will be slain by the brightness of His appearing. During the thousand years which follow this first resurrection the earth will remain uninhabited, and the demonic originator and instigator of all sin will live upon it. Conducted thither by a mighty angel,[78] and bound in "chains of darkness," [79] he will wander about with his fallen angelic companions. At this exhibition of the results of the rebellion against God which he had brought about, the watching universe will exclaim, "Is this the man that made the earth to tremble, that did shake the kingdoms; that made the world a wilderness, and destroyed the cities thereof; that opened not the house of his prisoners?"[80] The extent of the devil's work against God and His people will be clearly seen, and every being in the universe will realize the cost of rebellion against Heaven.

The dismissal of Azazel's goat almost completed the special rituals of the Day of Atonement. As Azazel's goat was being banished, the high priest burned the carcasses of his bull and the Lord's goat outside the camp and incinerated their fat on the altar.[81] This signaled that the cleansing of the sanctuary, and the saints, had been consummated.

The high priest then bathed and changed into his "golden garments"[82] and sacrificed his own and his people's burnt offerings of consecration,[83] as well as the seven lambs for the people's peace offerings.[84] At this juncture he offered the regular evening sacrifices.

Now, for the fourth and final time during the Day of Atonement the high priest entered the most holy place. Before he did this, he bathed and changed into his white robes and then went into the oracle to retrieve the censer of intercession which had been smoldering in the presence of God all day.[85] As he carried it through the holy place, the whole house "was filled with smoke."[86] To alert all the worshipers to the fact that mediation had ceased for "the Day" he flung the embers of incense at the foot of the altar of burnt offering[87] where the ashes were poured out. Again bathing and donning his "golden garments," he superintended the carrying out of the concluding tasks of this very special day.

The blood-splattered veil into the most holy place was removed by priestly hands, and a new one, woven by the women of Israel,[88] hung in its place. A symbol of the flesh of Jesus,[89] this pristine tapestry evokes glimpses of the incarnation and access to the throne by the Saviour. By this concluding ceremony the high priest restored the "cleansed" sanctuary "to its rightful state"[90] and signaled the beginning of an annual cycle of the festivals and services of redemption. At this point in the rituals, the privileges of the Jubilee were proclaimed by priestly trumpets every fifty years.[91]

The final act of the high priest at the conclusion of this day was to come forth from the holy precincts arrayed in his gorgeous robes, to bless God's joyous people.[92] On the hem of his blue robe hung golden bells, and as he moved, the worshipers rejoiced to hear "the joyful sound" of their golden tongues announcing that Israel's emancipation had been accomplished.[93]

And when our great High Priest, having completed His mediation in His heavenly sanctuary during the eschatological day of atonement, returns for His saints,[94] He will pronounce His "never-ending blessing"[95] on them. Then will commence the "jubilee, when the land should rest."[96] Israel's Day of Atonement ended with a banquet for the "satisfied" high priest and his jubilant friends.[97] This feast anticipated the "marriage supper of the Lamb,"[98] at which the Saviour's "friends"[99] join to praise Him, declaring, "all our *guilt* is Christ's."

Part II

The Priesthood

Preview

An artist cannot paint a rainbow, nor can a sculptor express a mother's love. Even through the symbols devised by God in the tabernacle and its furnishings, its complex system of sacrifices and comprehensive festivals, we see only cryptic, unfeeling shadow pictures of our Saviour's character.

In the court we observe the lamb burning on the altar, and in the laver remember the ghosts of donated mirrors containing cleansing water.

We continue into the holy place and imagine its gleaming walls and lovely tapestries, but our hearts only glimpse the Light of the world and smell the Bread of Life and breathe the air laden with the fragrance of His intercession.

Beyond the inner draperies we sense the oracle ablaze with glory, and in imagination see the cherubim standing on the mercy seat above the ark containing the law inscribed in rock, a living branch, and life-giving manna, all surrounded by shimmering radiance we cannot approach.

But our hearts feel that even these topological brush strokes of the Master Artist leave Christ's glorious portrait blurred and cold. This "glorious array" of the sanctuary[1] fails to convey His affectionate nature, and His tender concern. Our Saviour's understanding of the human condition and His compassion require a living type, for only a lover's voice can awaken his beloved's love.

To satisfy this need Jehovah called a man to serve, for only a living person can play the part of Him who ever lives. In Israel's priest, ordained by God to reveal the facets and framework of His Son's sovereign ministry of grace, we shall see Christ, our great High Priest.

Chapter 6

The Priest and High Priest

All my *needs* are Christ's

Priest is an abbreviation of the Greek *presbuteros*, an older man or elder, and suggests wisdom and experience. The Hebrew *cohen* means one who stands up for another and approaches God on his behalf, a prince or ruler of his family, a judge[1] in "matters of controversy within his gates."

To help us to grasp the uniqueness of our Saviour's priesthood, the Most High has left a glimpse of salvation's earliest priest. This Canaanite king reigned in righteousness and peace from his capitol in Old Salem and blessed the victorious Abraham, serving bread to feed his soul and wine to seal his covenant. Of this "order,"[2] Christ is our Covenant Maker and feeds us with His spiritual flesh and blood.

Melchisedek must needs have been a man[3] to understand humanity; and, to act as the sinner's Mediator, it was incumbent upon Jesus to assume human nature.[4] So Mary's womb was made the portal to His earthly life. Now He grasps the throne of God with His divine hand, and with His nail-marred human hand clasps His earth-bound brothers and sisters to His spear-pierced heart. Ancient priests sought to link men with God, but our High Priest is the one God-man.

Melchisedek and Jesus both lacked legal pedigrees[5] in the ancestral genealogies kept by Levite scribes. Like Habaiah's sons they should, "as polluted, [have been] put from the priesthood."[6] But anonymous and yielded to God's will, Melchisedek foreshadowed Him who, in obedience to His Father, serves His weary warriors, and from New Salem's hill holds out his broken body and spilled blood to satisfy man's spiritual hunger and thirst.

49

After man fell, God purposed that the first-born son should act as the family priest, but many shied away from this responsibility. So when Jehovah freed His people and led them to Horeb, He planned that every Israelite should constitute his "royal priesthood."[7] He summoned Moses to Sinai's brow to learn His curriculum for them, "for the priest's lips should keep knowledge, and they should seek the law at his mouth: for he is the messenger of the Lord."[8] But while the legislator studied with God on the mountain, his people apostatized in the valley and made, and then adored, a calf of gold! On returning, Moses was appalled at what he saw and smashed the tablets before the people to symbolize that they had broken the Eternal's law.

The fearless judge crushed the idol calf and made the culprits drink its dust to become the graveyard of their god! Standing before the renegades, he cried, "Who is on the Lord's side?" And "all the sons of Levi gathered themselves together unto him."[9] "Take the Levites instead of all the firstborn," the Lord decreed[10] and there and then honored them with the service of His tabernacle.[11] In answer to Moses' prayer, Aaron, who had acquiesced in sin, repented to become a "saint."[12] Forgiven most, he loved most fervently, and so God granted the priesthood to him and his descendants as a gift.[13] Officiating during their prime, from thirty to fifty years of age,[14] priests sought to understand and sympathize with the penitents so as to apply Heaven's saving balm to their sin-sick souls.[15]

Note the conditions surrounding the call to ministry. No man sought this office, and later, those who did so in arrogant rebellion against God's will perished miserably.[16] The Lord chose the men He wanted, and their responsibility was to heed the Voice and serve.[17] Jesus perfectly exemplified this attitude. He "glorified not himself to be made an high priest" but obeyed His Father's summons. And His priesthood is unique, for He is also the Victim. He became man to communicate with man and assumed mortality to die in his stead. And now He lives to plead the merits of His sacrifice for every repentant sinner. But observe the Lord's caution: "Whosoever . . . hath any blemish, let him not approach to offer the bread of his God."[18] This physical rule beams on Christ's character, for His righteousness is framed in law, and His perfection is crowned, "Holiness to the Lord."[19]

The priest's family must strive toward this ideal. The chastity of his wife[20] alerts us to the standard to be reached by the Christian "bride" of the celestial High Priest.[21] The priest must make his home where God decreed. During the years of wandering, the Levites formed the perimeter of the sacred square within which God's holy shrine was pitched, and were its guardians. In the Promised Land they were granted forty-eight cities, for the service of Jehovah was to be their inheritance.[22] Distributed among God's people, they were to exemplify their Master. Jesus, too, was without nest or resting place[23] and claimed no earthly heritage. Living among men, He showed them how to live. His service to His Father and His fellow men was His satisfying inheritance.

A ceremony set apart those whom the Spirit first "called," and each of its details directs us to the Saviour.[24] "Taken" by Heaven's choice, the priest was brought to the sanctuary as God's captive. Yielded to His Father's will, Christ submissively moved from eternity, through Bethlehem and Calvary, and back to His celestial sanctuary, His only delight was to obey.

The candidate then "stripped." This signaled that our Lord willingly laid aside His royal robes and kingly crown, and "emptied Himself" of the independent exercise of certain prerogatives of Deity to become one with mankind. Israel's priest, unable to cleanse himself, was "washed," literally baptized, by Moses, who stood in the place of God,[25] in water provided by the fountain opened in the smitten rock. The Son who submitted to His baptism of blood is mirrored in these humbling rites.

Now the sacerdotal wardrobe was flung open, and garments of glory and beauty,[26] prepared according to God's designs, of materials of His choosing, were freely provided. These clothes were to turn all hearts to the nature of Mary's Son. Linen, garnered from the fields of earth, was nourished by the dust. The relentless sickle then cut it down, the unremitting maul threshed its fibers, and the hot sun bleached them into snowy purity.[27] The spinner tortured them into threads, and the weaver's beam beat upon them, as a woman's hands fashioned the whitest lawn. All this pictured the development of the Man Christ Jesus, whose character was the white linen garment for His bride.

The mine yielded gold and precious stones. Fire melted and hammers shaped the metal into form, while the lapidary cut and disciplined the rocks into bright flowers of light. The self-less, innocent lamb provided wool, and rainbow dyes added color to distaff and loom. And from these substances, two kinds of material were woven. From these the Master designed the high priest's garments, tailoring them to suggest meaning to the pensive heart. "Everything connected with the apparel and deportment of the priests was to be such as to impress the beholder with a sense of the holiness of God, the sacredness of His worship, and the purity required of those who came into His presence."[28] Perfection and loveliness were pictured by these robes. Eternal Spirit, give us humility to read these signs aright.

White linen, symbol of Christ's righteousness,[29] first covered Aaron's nakedness. Breeches clothed his "loins," a term which describes man's "creative" faculties.[30] An enveloping coat with sleeves fell from his shoulders to his feet, with an embroidered sash bound about his waist.[31] This "girding" suggests his readiness to serve.[32] Finally a turban or miter draped his head.[33] These four snowy garments pictured the character of all priests as Christ's representatives and taught that His goodness must lie at the foundation of all ministry. Christ's "royal priests" must also posses His righteous character.

Three additional woolen pieces were needed for the regalia of the high priest. These symbolized what he *did,* in contrast with his white garments, which represented what he *was.* A sleeveless azure cloak, woven in one piece and reaching below the knees, was placed over his white coat.[34] Like the white of the linen garments, its blue color was significant, for scriptural colors have "work" to do.[35] To illustrate the ministry of this color, God designed cuffs and hems of blue ribbon as part of the distinctive dress[36] of all Israelites. This blue was to remind them of the commandments of God, because the Hebrews believed that the Lord had originally inscribed them with His finger on sapphire stones. Reflecting on these "borders of blue" they were to remember that the work of their hands and the steps of their feet must always remain within the circle of divine law. Woven in one piece, this azure symbol of obedience, resting on the foundation of white linen emblem of Christ's life of righteousness, must never be rent.[37]

A rich fringe of alternating woolen balls, shaped like pomegranates, and golden bells hung from the hem of the blue robe. The stuff of these pomegranates was blue, purple, and scarlet wool, similar to that used for the veils, and so reminiscent of Christ's humanity.[38] Did the seeds of these fruit appear as if bathed in blood to picture the fruitfulness of His life? And did the tongue of each bell testify to His golden fruit of faith that works by love? The high priest had but to stir, and their chorus carilloned the news to all: "He lives! He ministers!" But only by those who chose to cluster near was "his sound . . . heard when he goeth in unto the holy place before the Lord, and when he cometh out." [39]

From Olivet the Lord ascended to His Father with multitudes of blood-bought captive "first fruits." And following His inauguration as High Priest the golden bells of Pentecost rang out on wings of rushing winds to announce that He was ministering in His celestial temple. As the outgrowth of our Priest's righteousness, pictured by His white garments, and obedience, typified by His blue robe, sprang precious fruit and sweetest witness.

An ephod was worn over this sapphire cloak. From the high priest's shoulders this double apron of service reached to his knees, both back and front. Of the materials of the veils, this servant's livery pointed to the humanness and understanding of Christ's ministry. But this sign of service might be worn only upon the blue robe. Because of His life of perfect obedience, our High Priest is able to render acceptable service. Genuine ministry springs from compliance with God's call and is empowered by the grace of Christ's righteous life.

The ephod hung from gold-clasped onyx stones,[40] upheld by the priest's shoulders, signs of his strength.[41] Upon these two durable rocks the names of Israel's sons were etched according to their births, the six older on his right, the six younger on his left. Upon His shoulders our Good Shepherd bears home His lost-found sheep and lambs. What stories these gold-clasped rosters tell of comfort, encouragement, power, and strength! The name of every child of God is chiseled there. Is yours?

Around the ephod and above the high priest's heart, a sash of the materials of the veils was firmly wrapped.[42] John observed "the Son of man [as our High Priest] . . . girt about the paps [the word is feminine] with a golden girdle."[43] Child of God, your High Priest is ever prepared, "girded" with this sign of human love and understanding.

These seven vestments formed the backdrop for the foursquare "breastplate of judgment."[44] Bezaleel made this bejeweled symbol of the government of God out of material that emphasized the human nature of Jesus. This doubled piece of cloth, hung by gold chains from the onyx epaulets, was bound to them by ribbons of blue. Its form was square, measured by the high priest's span, for Christ's creative and redemptive hand encompasses and controls the justice of God. As your compassionate Judge, He holds you in the hollow of His hand, and neither demons nor men can pluck you from His grasp.

The borders of the breastplate were reenforced by golden braids enclosing twelve stones, three to a side, similar to the gems which gleam in the foundation of the apocalyptic city.[45] This governmental capital of the remade earth, like Israel's ancient encampment, and this breastplate on the high priest's heart, is planned foursquare. Around the sanctuary in the desert each tribe camped beside his standard and mustered in a hollow square, three to the side.[46] Named in the celestial city gates, these septs themselves were signs for "Abraham's seed," a term embracing saved souls everywhere.[47] John observed that these representative men have entrances to the city through designated tribal portals. To illustrate our High Priest's care, God's chosen ones were remembered by name both on the jewels in the breastplate resting on His heart of love, and carried in triumph on the onyx shoulder pieces of His strength.

Within the breastplate's jeweled borders, twelve similar stones were set in clasps of gold in rows of three, each inscribed with a tribal name, but now in the order of their march. God chose the rock foundation for each clan, and "each stone has its special significance, bearing its important message from God."[48] Let us try to decipher their story.

The stones signify Christ, our Rock. As these rainbow gems glow in the glory of the Shekinah, their substance reflects the light of the Sun of righteousness. His splendor passes through their hearts to enable them to let their "light so shine." The blue of the sapphire and agate testifies to God's law, while the gold of the topaz glows with "faith which works by love and purifies the soul."[49] The azure and gold mingle to sing of the verdant hope shining through the emerald, peridot, and jasper. The crimson ruby and the flesh-hued carnelian sob in anguish for the sins for which Christ's bloody death alone can make atonement. And when His carmine flesh was married to the blue of His obedience, men saw through the purple amethyst, the robe of the King-Priest. The onyx and the zircon are alight with snowy purity, while in the sardonyx the white and scarlet remain separate side by side, yet form a single stone. Each of the dozen rocks, pigmented with the hues and tints of the Light of the world, silently flashes its message from the breastplate, anticipating the splendor of the luminous ministry of the celestial High Priest in His work of judgment.

The substance of these jewels also had special significance. Seven stones traced their lineage to silica (common sand), while three were gendered by alumina, the clay around us. But, we ask, how can homely sand and common clay be transformed into beautiful gems? Alumina and silica still, the metamorphosed rocks, radiant with refracted and reflected light, are parables of Christ's transforming grace. The power of their Creator changed their earthiness to stardust. In some such mysterious manner sinful man becomes a child of light, and the bastard is adopted into the family of God.[50] Made lower than angels, the redeemed will sit with their Saviour on God's throne, as brothers and sisters of the King!

The substances of these precious crystals were made in solution. When conditions were right, crystals formed and gemstones were born. "Great waters" represent restless humanity in which people are tossed to and fro. In some such way, still indistinguishable in the floods of mankind surrounding them, sinners are touched by Heaven and transformed into saints. Crystals grow into their unique shapes according to the laws of their natures, and yet may be distorted if they develop too close to other crystals. Independence and space to grow are the secrets of their perfection. Christians, too, mature in grace and knowledge within the framework of their Creator's beneficent regulations.

The name of each tribe reflected the color of its jewel foundation. As these individual rays combined with the others, the fullness of purest light shone with a glory far beyond the single radiance of each stone. Like Aaron, our High Priest tenderly carries His lambs etched upon His heart, so that the glory of His church may flash into the darkness of this world. He plans soon to return to earth to complete His jewel collection.[51] Is your name now written on His breast? Is your light shining to glorify your Father?

To the right and left of these jeweled rosters, the Lord placed two stones of greater brilliancy, called Urim and Thummim.[52] The first sings of "light" to be joyfully followed, while the second whispers "Amen," quietly accepting God's denial. These messengers were to guide the nation as had the "cloud" and "fire" in the trackless desert. Today the Spirit's will, the "still, small voice," speaking in the heart of every Christian, fulfills the functions of these special gems.

And to complete the high priest's regalia, a golden crown, inscribed "Holiness to the Lord,"[53] was tied with a ribbon of blue in front of his snow white turban. Experience and wisdom were thus bound together by the sign of God's eternal law. This looked forward to our High Priest who one day will be crowned King of kings and Lord of lords.

The four garments of "fine linen clean and white" display Christ's *character* of perfect righteousness and call attention to what our High Priest *is* by nature. Upon this foundation His fivefold livery of *service* represents what He *does* for sinners. As members of His royal priesthood, we should inquire of ourselves how closely we are reaching His example. All this symbolic power was provided free to Aaron, and we, too, may receive the riches of His gift of grace.

Completely robed, the high priest was now ready for his consecration. Perfumed ointment was poured upon his head. This symbolized that "the crown of the anointing oil of his God is upon him."[54] This chrism streamed down Aaron's beard[55] and splashed upon the earth, illustrating the unstinted riches of God's gift of the Spirit on the Day of Pentecost. After He had set apart God's High Priest as the Minister in His celestial sanctuary, Heaven's Anointing Oil splashed upon this earth to fuel the cloven tongues of eloquent flame on each of the disciples prepared to receive Him. Christ's "kingdom of priests" was thus enabled to proclaim the gospel of salvation to all the world.

A ram of dedication then provided blood to mark the high priest's right ear, thumb, and toe.[56] These locations signaled that henceforth he would hear, work, and walk only where Calvary might direct. Upon this carmine authorization, oil was also put on ear, hand, and foot.[57] Thus through Golgotha's surrender and Pentecost's victory our High Priest was empowered to serve.

And as the climax of his consecration, Israel's high priest held out his hands to be "filled" with the slain lamb and broken bread.[58] The Hebrew for "consecrate" means "to fill the hands." These sacrificial gifts he presented to the people and then burned them upon the altar as a tribute to God. And now, in their ultimate fulfillment, these venerable rites have reached reality in our High Priest's offerings of His body and blood to His Father and to us.

Connected with the consecration of the high priest was the dedication of the tabernacle.[59] These combined ceremonies pointed to the inauguration of Christ our High Priest, and the dedication of His heavenly sanctuary as taking place on one occasion.

All these types focus on Jesus. His ear listens to His Father's voice, Spirit quickened. His hands, bloodied by the nails, work for His Father's kingdom, Spirit directed. His feet leave crimson footsteps, marking our way to glory, Spirit lighted. O Father, how we love Him for His love!

In imagination watch our High Priest mediating for us day by day. The gates into His temple are wide open. Upon His loving heart and strong shoulders He bears His sheep and lambs on jeweled foundations and knows them each by name. His hands hold out the bread of life to feed their souls. He meets me where I am, and I know that all my *needs* are Christ's. The day of His intercession is fast drawing to a close and His voice urgently calls, "Is it nothing to you?"

Part III
The Feasts of the Lord
Preview

The Lord is concerned with how His people spend their time. At Creation He required that mankind cease ordinary labor on the seventh day of each week. In the Promised Land He legislated that Israel should consider the first day of each month, New Moon Day, as a time for relaxation and communion with Heaven. Two of these new moons, of Nisan and Tishri, He ordained as "New Year's Days," providing His people with opportunities to review their past and plan for their future. The former marked the commencement of the religious year for the sacred feasts, and the latter the civil year for business transactions.

During the first month, Nisan, besides the Feast of the New Moon, the Passover occurred on the fourteenth, followed by its week-long Feast of Unleavened Bread, which included the presentation of the Wave Sheaf of the first fruits of barley on the sixteenth. Fifty days from this offering of grain came Pentecost. These three celebrations constituted the spring or early festive cycle.

After Pentecost there followed four months of summer, during which God's people observed only Sabbaths and new moons. On the first of the seventh month, Tishri, the civil calendar commenced. This important new moon, called the Feast of Trumpets or Rosh Hashana, announced the coming of the Day of Atonement at the end of the "ten days of penitence." Five days following this, from the fifteenth to the twenty-second, the Feast of Tabernacles climaxed the annual cycle. These three seventh-month gatherings were the autumnal or "end festivals." In connection with the feasts, the Lord added seven ceremonial Sabbaths to be observed as were the weekly Sabbaths.

Every Seventh year was to be regarded as semi-sabbatic. The land was to be left fallow and certain servitors freed. And to climax the entire religious epoch, the Lord decreed that every fiftieth year should be a Jubilee. Within this time frame God worked out His plan for the salvation of the lost world.

Of the three spring festivals, Ellen White noted: "These types were fulfilled, not only as to the event, but as to the time,"[1] and added: "In like manner the types which relate to the second advent must be fulfilled at the time pointed out in the symbolic service."[2]

Chapter 7

Feasts of New Moons and Trumpets

All my *times* are Christ's

The New Moon was Israel's most frequent festival, celebrated at home and in places of local assembly, while special sacrifices were offered at the sanctuary. Included among Paul's "shadows of things to come," it pointed to realities in Christ's ministry.

Since Scripture often represents the first part as standing for the whole, the ceremonies dedicating the new moon consecrated the month. The priest's proclamation, "It is sanctified!" announced this, and the monthly banquet provided opportunity for each family to adore the Controller of the annual cycle.[1] Its Hebrew name, *rosh chodesh*, suggesting renewal and freshness, is also translated "month".

The Lord chose several ways to call attention to His control of time. The Sabbath pointing to Him as Creator, provided weekly leisure for worship and the study of His wonderful works. Each month the never-failing crescent illustrated the Sustainer's predictability and faithfulness. Commencing as a silver sliver and waxing to full-orbed splendor, the moon displays the modest beginning and gradual expansion of the kingdom of heaven. Dependent on the sun for its orbit and light, it cautions us that "apart from Christ we are like an unkindled taper, like the moon when her face is turned away from the sun; we have not a single ray of brightness to shed into the darkness of the world. But when we turn toward the Sun of Righteousness, when we come in touch with Christ, the whole soul is aglow with the brightness of the divine presence."[2]

But while the moon lights the traveler for only a few nights, the "Light of the world" never withdraws His presence from His faithful pilgrims. Precise, regular, predictable, and modest, it illustrates Heaven's unchanging law, and "to the heart softened by the grace of God . . . the moon . . . utter[s its] words of counsel and advice."[3] As he contemplates "the solemn glories of the moon,"[4] the Christian joins the Israelite in sensing that the interdependent purposes of Providence precisely progress toward their designed goals for blessing mankind and glorifying Heaven.

The Creator did not wish astronomical calculations to take the place of the living, expectant observation of His people. The Hebrew sages record that eyewitnesses were to fix the time of every new moon. In similar vein, Jesus warned His disciples against trying to figure out the day and hour of His coming, but urged instead that they remain continually on the "watch." The subjects of His kingdom must personally read the signs and testify to what they see. Each month observers hastened to the sanctuary to report the "silver bow new-bent in heaven," and a banquet was provided to encourage the first witnesses.[5]

Following the captivity, the Sanhedrin met in the Hall of Polished Stones on the eve of the twenty-ninth of each month, to await the sighters.[6] Charts of the appearance of the crescent had been developed, and these were used to check the evidence.[7] When two had agreed, and the interlocutors were satisfied, the festival was announced. But should no credible evidence be forthcoming, the day was reckoned to the previous month, which was then described as "full," i. e. of thirty days.[8] On the following evening the sickle moon was easily seen, and the chief of the court announced the new month with the formula, "It is sanctified!" to which the people responded, "It is sanctified! It is sanctified!" Then the ram's horn shofar proclaimed that the regular month had commenced.

The new moon of Nisan marked the beginning of the religious year,[9] while the new moon of the month Tishri, the seventh month of the sacred calendar, was New Year's Day for the Hebrew civil almanac, and was regarded as the most important of the New Moon festivals. It was called the Feast of Trumpets because two silver bugles were sounded in addition to the shofars.[10] For this special feast the priests who played them were flanked by others with goat's horns. "The shophar blew a long note and the trumpets a short one."[11] The rabbis believed that the call of these silver trumpets commemorated creation, when they had played an obligato to the song of "the morning stars" and the shout of "the sons of God."[12] The word *shout* means "to exult,"[13] rejoice,[14] blow a festive trumpet,[15] or celebrate."[16]

The Lord stipulated that only priests should sound the shofar. Made of a large ram's horn with a silver mouthpiece and used for ordinary New Moon feasts, it produced a dull and heavy sound which carried long distances. For the Feast of Trumpets, the shofar was the horn of a wild goat with a mouthpiece of gold. The manner of blowing was a sustained blast, followed by a quavering one, and then a sustained sound held three times as long as the quavering one. These three phrases were sounded thrice.[17]

The trumpets were made of a "whole" piece of silver,[18] perhaps to emphasize completeness and freedom from fracture. Used in Scripture for the redemptive half shekel presented for the firstborn,[19] as well as for the foundations of the tabernacle building,[20] silver is a symbol of obedience.[21] The silver trumpets sounded Heaven's call for full submission and reminded the perceptive Israelites of the summons to Sinai to learn God's law and the need for strict obedience to His precepts.

The priests were required to sound well-defined notes[22] by setting the instruments to their lips[23] and blowing,[24] acts which indicate personal involvement. Jewish sages noted that New Year's trumpet calls were to awaken the people from spiritual lethargy and appeal for repentance[25] in face of the approaching Day of Atonement, with the reminder that Sinai's law was the basis of the judgment.

The new moon of the seventh month was called "a day of blowing," because trumpets were to be blown from morning until evening by priests organized in relays. The people who were able obeyed the psalmist's command, "Blow up the trumpet in the new moon,"[26] adding their personal witness to the sacerdotal call.

The New Year's trumpets pealed the knell of the departed year, and inquired with tongues of "choicest silver."[27] "What has been its record of your life? Repent!" They then heralded a new epoch, "Life was; but life is, and life shall be! Stay alert!" And thus they prepared Israel for the Day of Atonement.

The accurate timing of the new moon of the first month, Nisan or Abib, was vital for the start of the entire religious calendar, for on it hinged not only the dates of the three spring festivals, but also the timing of the three autumnal, or "end festivals."[28] At the conclusion of Israel's religious cycles the Sabbatic year and the jubilee were both reckoned from the New Moon. In the beginning the Creator had designed the moon to "rule," and its kingdom was time.

At each new moon the sound of a "trumpet was heard, summoning the people to meet with God"[29] to dedicate the month with its hope and possibilities. The Lord promised to listen and take the case of each one of His people "in remembrance."

Remember always means to hear with a view toward doing something.[30] The expressions "memorial of blowing" [31] and "day of blowing"[32] were understood to signify that God was being reminded of the needs of His people. With this in mind, Isaiah described the faithful as "the Lord's remembrancers," [33] and the angel explained to Cornelius that his prayers and alms had reached heaven as a "memorial" or reminder of his character.[34] The thief on the cross understood this concept in his petition, "Lord, remember me when thou comest into thy kingdom." [35]

But the call of the shofars and trumpets was heard only by those living close to the house of God. To ensure that the proclamation reached every Israelite, a great torch was lighted on the summit of Olivet.[36] This signaled the news to watchers on other strategic hills, who kindled their beacons. In a few moments the country from end to end was flooded with light, "like a sea of fire."[37] The Lord's design that His people should unite in adoration and fellowship was thus fulfilled.

Pagan new year celebrations were characterized by ribald mirth and drunken revelry, but the trumpet called God's people to commemorate the Creator's providences with solemn joy and rededication based on sacrifice. While all New Moon feasts were holy convocations,[38] requiring attendance at local places of worship, only the Feast of Trumpets was to be observed as a sabbath. Additional sacrifices of a bull, a ram, and seven lambs for burnt offerings of consecration, with their appropriate meal and drink offerings, and a kid for a sin offering were added to the daily presentations. This additional blood stressed that true joy rests upon the Substitute's death. While the priest was pouring the libation of wine on the altar during the morning service, the Levite choir sang Psalm 81; then at the evening service they chanted Psalm 29.

The rabbis considered the new moon a special occasion for women. God designed that Eve "should possess neither inferiority nor superiority to the man, but that in all things she should be his equal. The holy pair were to have no interest independent of each other; and yet each had an individuality in thinking and acting. But after Eve's sin, as she was first in the transgression, the Lord told her that Adam should rule over her. She was to be in subjection to her husband, and this was a part of the curse. In many cases the curse has made the lot of woman very grievous and her life a burden. . . . Infinite wisdom devised the plan of redemption, which places the race on a second probation by giving them another trial."[39] Because of sin, the gate of Paradise was barred by flaming light, and the tree of life placed beyond the reach of "divorced" Adam and Eve and their descendants. But the Gardener has worked out His grand design to restore an even more lovely Eden to His ransomed and reinstated "bride" in the land where there will be "no more curse."[40]

The women of Israel were released from their duties on the new moon and might spend the day as they wished, perhaps by offering a sacrifice, if they lived near the sanctuary[41] or by visiting a prophet.[42] The rabbis point to their faithfulness in refusing gold for Sinai's idol calf[43] as another reason for this privilege.

The Revelator's prediction of the monthly pilgrimage of "the Lamb's wife" to the celestial city is draped in precious promises. From God's throne, an emblem of His beneficent government, flows the stream whose waters bestow unending life, and He calls to her, "Come and drink!" On the banks of the river grows the tree whose monthly fruit, in a dozen varieties, supplies eternal vigor, and His voice invites her, "Freely eat!" In response, the virgin saints[44] stream through the pearly gates into the presence of the Bridegroom Lamb each month[45] to rest and feast, and to worship and love. Then "there shall be no more curse,"[46] and Eden's sentence will be forever reversed. Israel's Feast of the New Moon was typical of this healing event.

Around these family festivals clustered cherished memories filled with "mirth."[47] On a new moon David's father presented a sacrifice of thanksgiving, urging every member of his family to be present.[48] On a new moon Saul arranged a banquet for his kin and favored guests, at which his son-in-law David would be missed because his seat was empty.[49] New Moon feasts were occasions for reunion and times for sharing spiritual and social blessings with family and friends.

Around these national festivals clustered rich, historical memories. On a new moon the tabernacle was erected[50] and the twelve tribes pledged their allegiance to God, joyously enumerated their pedigrees,[51] and discovered that the family of Jacob was intact! On a new moon Levi responded to the Lord's call to sanctuary service as an example of what every citizen should be.[52] On a new moon Aaron trudged up the heights of Hor to die, testifying to his trust and resignation.[53] On a new moon Hezekiah reconsecrated Yahweh's defiled temple,[54] presaging One greater who would someday dedicate His celestial temple. The feasts of the joyous moon stand as silver mileposts shimmering down the path of salvation's story.

Prophets invested New Moon feasts with overtones of eschatology and understood that the trumpet's call was to judgment.[55] In the fullness of time the gospel trumpet[56] alerted the earth to what was about to happen in the celestial sanctuary on the final day of atonement[57] and pointed God's people to the judgment they faced.[58] From the psalms[59] the rabbis concluded that on the Feast of Trumpets three books were opened by the Judge in preparation for the Day of Atonement. The "book of life" contains the names of those whose deeds God approves, while the "book of death" records evildoers. The third book remembered those whose cases were to be decided. They believed that the text, "He fashioneth their hearts alike; he considereth all their works"[60] focuses on the Feast of Trumpets.[61] Following this trumpet alert the people were granted "ten days of penitence" to prepare for the Day of Atonement.

Christ's trumpetlike voice had summoned His newly freed people to commune with Him in the glory of Mount Sinai. Egyptian darkness encased their minds until Heaven's light, garbed in law, both moral and ceremonial, exposed their need and displayed heaven's remedy. The trumpet called, "Obey and live; dawn brightens! Disobey, and darkness drowns! The covenant of works is a broken scaffold by which to erect the temple of salvation. Gather under the banner inscribed, 'I am Jehovah your God.'" But because too many of God's ancient people had refused Christ's voice speaking at Sinai, Paul warned his Hebrew Christian friends, "See that ye refuse not him that speaketh" now![62] "Blessed is the people that know the trumpet sound: they walk, O Lord, in the light of thy countenance."[63]

The New Moon will be the communal festival of the redeemed in the earth made new. The hosts of the saved will gather to reminisce on the precious chapters of their lives. On new moons the celestial "tabernacle of God [will once again be] with men, and he will dwell with them . . . and be their God," [64] and the ransomed tribes will enumerate their lineage[65] and Christ's "royal priests" perform their ceaseless eucharistic ministry. On new moons jubilant Aaron will scale the heights of Zion to sing the song with Moses; and the heavenly temple, "cleansed" and "restored to its rightful state" by a Greater than Hezekiah, will display the wonders of the Lamb as the focus of the universe. On new moons the translated bride, face to face with Jesus her husband, will view the past, the present, and the future, irradiated with the light of His glorious love.

The New Moon will be the family festival of the redeemed. On new moons each household will wend its happy path to the golden city[66] to hear Jesus extend His invitation to eat the fruit of the tree of life and drink of the waters of the river of peace. What stories of victory they will then tell! What memories of the ministry of grace will then flood their minds and sing on their tongues! But as triumphant Israel recounts its pedigree, will each family be complete? And when the King invites His ransomed kin to the feast of the joyous moon, will some son or daughter be missed because his or her setting at the silver table is vacant? As we prepare for that day, we still can say, "All our *times* are Christ's."

Chapter 8

Feasts of Passover and Unleavened Bread

All my *protection* is Christ's

While in Egypt the Israelites were forbidden to practice their religion. But as deliverance neared,[1] Moses asked Pharaoh's permission to offer a national sacrifice to Jehovah. He was peremptorily refused. The Lord then instructed him to demand that the king free the Hebrews, or face the consequences. But even nine catastrophic plagues failed to move the stubborn ruler. These evidences of Heaven's power over Egyptian deities, however, prepared the Israelites for something portentous.

At this juncture God directed the head of each family to sacrifice a lamb, and, with a bunch of hyssop, splash its blood on the door posts and lintel of his home, promising, "When I see the blood, I will pass over you."[2] This sign ensured that during the night of judgment the angel of death would spare the firstborn who remained within his blood-marked home.

The details of this initial Passover are instructive. "Egypt"[3] was in ferment, with its atheistic and defiant king bent on Israel's destruction. The Hebrews, on the other hand, were prepared for their freedom, and following the crimson signal and the midnight meal, started on their journey to the Promised Land. Thereafter God made the annual Passover a reenactment of this thrilling event and ordered the sacred calendar of His people to start with this month.[4] This festival eventually became the best attended of Israel's three religious pilgrimages.[5]

In Palestine the timing of the Passover hinged on the ripeness of barley. God required that the festal banquet on the fourteenth of Abib, the earing month,[6] also called Nisan,[7] should be followed on the sixteenth, or "third day," by the presentation at the altar of a sheaf of ripe grain.[8] As the season approached, priests examined the fields to ascertain whether a sheaf of barley would be ready. If they deemed this possible, the new moon prior to this "wave offering" marked the beginning of Nisan. But should they decide that the grain would not be ripe, a thirteenth month was added to the previous year,[9] and a full moon later the barley would, of course, be ready for the sickle. This timing based on ripening grain had overtones of both mercy and judgment, as did the Divine "Passing over" to investigate the obedience of His people. The Passover thus not only commemorated the Exodus, it also anticipated "the last days" and the final harvest of "sealed" souls purchased by the blood of the true Paschal Lamb.

For fifteen centuries each household selected its perfect yearling male lamb or kid on the tenth of Nisan, and tethered for all to see it, ready for its killing on the fourteenth.[10] This was done so that its appearance might cause conversation about the marvelous deliverance from Egypt, for the male animal represented the firstborn. In the final year of Christ's ministry the fourteenth of Nisan fell on "Good" Friday.

On the previous Sabbath, "six days before the passover,"[11] Jesus enjoyed a quiet meal in the home of Lazarus, Martha, and Mary. The next day, Palm Sunday, the ninth of Nisan, He rode triumphantly to Jerusalem on a donkey, pausing on the brow of Olivet to weep over the city and its doomed people.[12] That night, "when the fast westering sun should pass from sight in the heavens, Jerusalem's day of grace would be ended."[13] Sundown marked the beginning of the tenth of Nisan. That night, in plenary session, the illegally summoned Sanhedrin condemned Heaven's Paschal Lamb to death, and by their decision "the doom of Jerusalem should be forever sealed."[14] Jesus was thus appointed to die on the very day the paschal lamb was chosen, and the prophetic type met its Antitype.

During the four days following, the Jewish rulers plotted with Judas to ensure the carrying out of Caiaphas's suggestion that His death should not take place "on the feast day, lest there be an uproar among the people."[15] But Satan's clever scheme to frustrate a further prophetic type miscarried. Once embarked on a course of sin, man is no longer in control; a tyrant has taken charge.

The rubric required that the paschal lamb should be kept "until the fourteenth day of the same month: and the whole assembly of the congregation of Israel shall kill it in the evening."[16] The most powerful representative body of the Hebrew nation, which included priests, rulers, scribes, and lawyers, joined by the common people, Herod, the tetrarch of Galilee, and supported by the Roman governor and soldiers, united in crucifying the Saviour,[17] and the day this deed was done was Friday, the fourteenth of Nisan![18] Type thus met Antitype as "Christ our passover is sacrificed for us."[19] The precision of this typological prediction is awe inspiring.

The paschal lamb was to be slaughtered "in the evening," a Hebrew phrase meaning "between the evenings."[20] Many suggestions have been made, but no final conclusion has been reached as to the significance of this expression. In Gesenius's discussion of the wide range of possible meanings is one which states that the lamb might be slaughtered any time after 12:01 noon on the thirteenth, when the "evening" of the fourteenth actually began, through sunset on the fourteenth, when "the evening" ended. If this thirty-hour period is accepted, it accommodates both the time of Christ's participation in the Upper Room during our Thursday evening[21] and that of the Pharisees later on Friday.[22] It also provides time for Josephus's statement that 240,000 lambs were slaughtered at the Passovers during the days of Christ. And so on the afternoon of the thirteenth Jesus requested two of His disciples to sacrifice the lamb at the temple and prepare the paschal meal, and about sunset joined them in carrying out the age-old customs.[23] Our Lord thus placed the stamp of His approval on the ceremonies He had long before devised, and by His life and example fulfilled their intent.

The law stipulated that all leaven should be removed from every home. The head of each family would deliberately plant pieces of leaven in strategic places in his house, and, accompanied by his children, carried out his ceremony before the fourteenth of Nisan.[24] With lighted candle, he searched every nook and cranny, explaining what he was doing, and thus fulfilled the prediction, "I will search Jerusalem with candles."[25] This prohibition against leaven extended for the seven days of the Feast of Unleavened Bread[26] and called attention to the need to search out all harmful principles with the help of the "candle" of Scripture[27] and to remove them from the hearts of the worshipers.

Leaven was fermented dough which, when added to fresh meal, caused it to rise. In Scripture leaven is used as a symbol of any principle which, working from within, silently and continuously influences the nature of whatever it permeates. The context indicates clearly whether leaven represents good or evil ideas.[28]

Using leaven as an illustration, the Saviour inveighed against sins which characterized many people of His day. "Beware of the leaven of the Pharisees," He warned, referring to their "doctrine which,"[29] He explained was "hypocrisy,"[30] a philosophy compounded with religiosity, the "product of self-seeking. The self glorification was the object of their lives. . . . Among the followers of our Lord today, as of old, how widespread is this subtle, deceptive sin!"[31] The Pharisees were sticklers for the letter of the law and separatists from all whom they considered sinners. Among, them, however, were men of the highest ideals.

The "leaven of the Sadducees"[32] was materialism. These liberals chose not to believe in the supernatural or in angels,[33] and were virtual atheists. They arrested and scourged some of the disciples for proclaiming Christ's resurrection[34] and were disturbed to discover that men were actually demon possessed.[35] They ignored prayer and denied the Divine authority of the Old Testament, except for the books of Moses, and even questioned parts of these.[36] Opposing the traditions of the Pharisees, they refused to accept the ideas of future punishments or rewards. Because "It is expedient!"[37] was their motto, they united with the Pharisees to procure Christ's crucifixion. Jesus was, however, more scathing against the hypocritical Pharisee than the liberal and secular Sadducee.

"The leaven of Herod"[38] was another of our Lord's targets. Herod means "hero" or "he-man." While several Herods are mentioned in the New Testament, the attitude of each toward Christ was similar, and so we shall consider the Herodian character as a composite. "Herod" was a foreign ruler with leanings toward Rome, seeking to govern the Jews by force. The blackness of his heart was exposed by his treatment of the babes of Bethlehem and John the Baptist.[39] Self-willed and sensual, proud and cruel, he finally yielded his integrity to the whim of a wanton. "Herod will kill thee"[40] describes his attitude toward the Saviour, and when finally confronted by Him, he was "amused."[41]

Pharisaic religiosity, Sadducaic liberalism, and Herodian brutality were alike denounced by Jesus. "These false principles, when once accepted, worked like leaven in the meal, permeating and transforming the character."[42] Only after the removal of the leaven of the old life could the wonder of the Paschal Sacrifice be understood and the "flesh" and "blood" of the Son of God appropriately "eaten" and "drunk." And to teach these lessons, leaven was symbolically removed from each home in preparation for the Passover. The message of this rite was, "Let every one that nameth the name of Christ depart from iniquity."[43]

When the four days of the "showing forth" of Christ, the true Paschal Lamb, ended on Friday the fourteenth of Nisan, "He was oppressed, and he was afflicted . . . : he is brought as a lamb to the slaughter, and as a sheep before her shearers is dumb, so he openeth not his mouth . . . He was cut off out of the land of the living: for the transgression of my people was he stricken."[44] Paul explained that paschal blood typified "the precious blood of Christ, as of a lamb without blemish and without spot."[45]

The law required that the paschal lamb be flawless so as to represent the Saviour, who is "holy, harmless, undefiled, separate from sinners."[46] Defenseless and unresisting,[47] patient and loving,[48] harmless and submissive,[49] the lamb was easily slaughtered.

In the Egyptian Passover the blood had been sprinkled on the doorjambs and lintel of each home by the father of the family.[50] But in the Palestinian rite the victim was sacrificed at the sanctuary by the householder or a Levite[51] and its blood splashed on the altar of burnt offering by a priest.[52] "Door" suggests a gateway for going out or coming in and illustrates the decision-making faculty of the heart, for "out of it are the issues of life."[53] And "so the merits of Christ must be applied to the soul."[54] Calling our attention to this ritual Ellen White cries, "Lift up Jesus before the people. Strike the door-posts with the blood of Calvary's Lamb, and you are safe."[55]

Throughout the week following the Passover only unleavened bread might be eaten.[56] These seven days suggest the completeness of man's earthly pilgrimage, and their message still is:

"Serve [the Lord] in sincerity and in truth."[57] In this context Paul warned, "Know ye not that a little leaven leaventh the whole lump? Purge out therefore the old leaven, that ye may be a new lump, as ye are unleavened." Since "Christ our Passover is sacrificed for us: . . . let us keep the feast, not with old leaven, neither with the leaven of malice and wickedness; but with the unleavened bread of sincerity and truth."[58] "The use of unleavened bread also was significant. The leaven of sin must be put away from all who would receive life and nourishment from Christ." [59] The paschal cakes were called "the bread of affliction" to remind the participants that they had left Egypt "in haste," [60] driven out, and had then wandered for years in hardship.[61]

In Egypt a bunch of hyssop had been used to sprinkle blood. Hyssop, an illustration of humility as well as cleansing, was used in the ceremonies of the red heifer and the two sparrows.[62] God used it here to keep before His people the truth that the simplest of means may apply His Son's redeeming blood to needy hearts. It was not enough for the neighbor's home to be thus marked; every household must provide the blood ransom for its own firstborn.[63] The lesson is clear, the Sacrifice of Calvary must be accepted personally by each member of the family of God.

But in Jerusalem the paschal blood was splashed on the altar in the court of the sanctuary, and portions of the animal burnt thereon.[64] Only then might the lamb be roasted whole to represent "the completeness of Christ's sacrifice."[65] After the lamb was skinned and cleaned, a shaft of pomegranate wood was pushed through its body, with a shorter stick, forcing open its rib cage.[66] Y-shaped branches were driven into the ground at each end of the fire pit, and the long shaft cradled in them. Upon this cross-spit the carcass was slowly rotated directly over the burning logs and roasted.[67] For fifteen centuries this tableau pictured the immolation of the Lamb of God upon the cross.

God forbade the breaking of any of the lamb's bones,[68] and John noted the fulfillment of this type.[69] The skeletal framework of Christ's suffering humanity, His law, and His covenant with His Father survived His ordeal intact.[70]

Each member of Israel's households was to eat of the roasted lamb.[71] The Passover is called a "sacrifice,"[72] the technical term used to describe the peace offering; and like it, the paschal victim must be eaten the same day it was slain to seal the covenant with Jehovah. "Eating" illustrated the truth that each worshiper must individually feed on the Messiah's "flesh." Jesus explained this as accepting His words and imitating His life.[73] He desires all His followers to thus be partakers of His experience.[74]

Unleavened bread was also part of this meal. The Israelites were to eat, as well as observe this *mazzoth*.[75] "Jesus used bread as a figure to illustrate the vitalizing power of his Spirit. The one sustains physical life, while the other satisfies the heart, and strengthens the moral powers."[76] Since "Christ our passover is sacrificed for us," Paul reasoned, "therefore let us keep the feast."[77] The apostle based salvation on the redeeming blood of Jesus and explained that it is sustained by feeding on His flesh and blood.

"Unleavened" or unfermented grape juice was drunk at this meal to complete the *mincah*. Only the pure "blood of grapes" could typify the blood of the Saviour untouched by corruption. The unfermented wine and unleavened bread both taught that "the leaven of sin must be put away from all who would receive the life and nourishment from Christ."[78] These types pointed to the keeping and preserving aspects of the Messiah's ministry, for "the Saviour has power to finally raise from the dead all those who, by faith, eat of his flesh and drink of his blood. This spiritual food gives to the believers a well-founded hope of the resurrection to immortal life in the kingdom of God."[79]

A salad of "bitter herbs" or wild endive[80] was eaten with the meal. This bitter flavor was deliberately added, not to be submerged in the tastes of the lamb and bread, but strong enough to remind the Israelites of the cruel "bitterness" of their Egyptian bondage[81] and the hardships of their wilderness wanderings.[82] These acrid leaves might be made into a pungent sauce into which the bread might be dipped.[83] "So when we feed on Christ, it should be with contrition of heart, because of our sins."[84]

In the Egyptian Passover the celebrants had stood to eat, loins girded, sandals on their feet, and staves in their hands, ready to march. These preparations focused on what lay beyond their meal. As soon as they had dined they were delivered from their Egyptian oppressors and were off.[85] Nourished by this food they were strengthened for their arduous march to the Promised

Land. God's role was clearly emphasized, "When I see the blood, I will pass over you." [86] But in Christ's day, the Passover was eaten at leisure in Jerusalem. The picture of John reclining on the Saviour's breast portrays the fact that the Redeemer had provided "rest" for His weary pilgrims and a haven for the tempest tossed.[87] When the meal had been completed, the unused elements were to be destroyed by fire." [88]

On the second day of the Feast of Unleavened Bread, the sixteenth of Nisan, a sheaf of ripe barley was harvested and presented to the Lord.[89] This took place on the day following the first ceremonial sabbath, the fifteenth, whatever day of the week it might occur. The sixteenth was thus always "the third day" after the sacrifice of the paschal lamb, and the phrase pointed to the presentation of the wave sheaf of "first fruits."

In Christ's time a field of barley near Jerusalem was cultivated for this rite, and at the proper time three men, provided with sickles and baskets, were directed to reap the sheaf. In the presence of witnesses three shocks of barley were cut and bound into one sheaf.[90] Carried solemnly to the temple, it was handed to one of "Aaron's sons" who stood before the great altar. He then waved it before the Lord, up to His throne and down to this earth to His priest, and then to the offerer.[91] This sheaf, which represented the first fruits of Israel's harvest, was thus consecrated to the Giver of all good gifts by these gestures. After accepting it, God returned it to sustain and bless His worshipers. Not until this ceremony had been carried out were the farmers to gather in their crops.

Jesus warned His disciples that one day He would suffer, be crucified, and rise "the third day."[92] Since He was the Paschal Lamb, this should have alerted them to the fact that His resurrection would take place on the very day on which the first fruits were presented. The sheaf of barley symbolized both the risen Saviour, and "the firstfruits of them that slept."[93] This type met its Antitype on Sunday, the sixteenth of Nisan, when Jesus did indeed rise from the grave on the "the third day," the "morrow after the sabbath."[94]

In the year of His death this first ceremonial sabbath of the paschal octave happened to fall on a weekly Sabbath. Following His own resurrection, Christ raised "many bodies of the saints which slept"[95] to be displayed as trophies before His Father and the universe. Taking these with Him to heaven at His ascension forty days later, "He present[ed] to God the wave sheaf, those raised with Him as representatives of that great multitude who shall come forth from the grave at His second coming."[96] Jesus Himself the antitypical Wave Sheaf, the first to be garnered from the fields of the world, presented Himself before His Father in the celestial sanctuary, and thus guaranteed the resurrection of the righteous in the final harvest at the end of the world.

During His last Passover, Jesus instituted the Lord's Supper as the initiatory banquet of fellowship for His church under the new covenant, and the prelude to the redemption of the world. "The observance of the Passover began with the birth of the Hebrew nation"[97] and ended with the birth of the Christian church. As we celebrate our Communion services, we should remember the ancient types and focus our attention on the victory they offer us on our journey to the Promised Land.

Jesus' last recorded act as He concluded the paschal meal was to lead His disciples in singing hymns of praise to His Father, and thus encouraging them to hope.[98] These psalms had been chanted for centuries by faithful celebrants and had sustained God's people in their troubles and victories. Now on the Saviour's lips they rang with the note of ultimate triumph.

The Lord had urged the fathers and mothers of Israel to use the opportunity provided by the paschal octave to instruct their children.[99] When asked, "What mean ye by this feast?" parents were to extol the Lord for what He had done for their ancestors, and then to explain all He was prepared to do for them now. The purpose of the banquet year by year was to call Israel's attention to the sprinkled blood, the sustaining meal, the covenant fellowship, and the supportive ministry of the Messiah, who was ready to bring transforming power into the hearts and lives of all who believed.[100] Jesus, as the Everlasting Father, complied with this ancient suggestion. He displayed in the symbols of the Communion Service the essence of the paschal rites, and by them pointed His sons and daughters of every age to their final fruition in the realized hope of the earth made new. And as we move on to that glorious consummation, let us express our confidence that "all our *protection* is Christ's."

Chapter 9
Feast of Pentecost

All my *gifts* are Christ's

The Feast of Pentecost was the second of Israel's three religious convocations. For just this one day all the men, as well as any others who were able, traveled to the sanctuary.[1] Some might need to journey for several days. Paul, for instance, set out from far away Macedonia, and "hasted, if it were possible for him, to be at Jerusalem the day of Pentecost,"[2] a trip needing several weeks of hard and dangerous travel.

More names have been given to this feast than to any other of Israel's festivals. Four expressions, Feast of Weeks,[3] Feast of the Fiftieth Day, or The Fiftieth translated into Greek as Pentecost,[4] remember the seven weeks and a day which elapsed between the presentation of the "wave sheaf" of barley on the sixteenth Nisan and the "wave loaves" of wheat on the sixth of Sivan. The Feast of Harvest[5] and The Day of First Fruits[6] commemorate this oblation. The rabbis termed *Shavout* The Feast of the Conclusion because it brought to an end the grain harvests of Palestine. They also called it The Season of the Giving of our Law because they believed that on this earliest national convocation after the exodus the decalogue had been presented on Mount Sinai.[7] Each of the three annual gatherings was a "solemn assembly"[8] and a unique harvest festival. The first fruits of barley were offered to the Lord on the sixteenth of Nisan, "the third day" after the paschal lamb had been slain. Precisely fifty days from this, on the Day of Pentecost, the first fruits of wheat, in the form of two loaves of leavened bread, were "waved" as a gift to the Lord. Celebrating the harvest of wine and oil, as well as the fruits of orchard and vineyard, the third festival was called the Feast of Tabernacles. These three "harvests" were types of periodic crises, or times of judgment, which move through the seasons of human life toward the close of probation, "the end of the world," or the final harvest.

The close and unshakable link between the "wave sheaf" and the "wave loaf" underlined the truth that Pentecost was rooted to the Passover. The Passover commemorated Israel's emancipation from Egypt, while Pentecost celebrated the giving of the law at Sinai and the organization of Israel as God's covenant people into a nation of "kings and priests."[9] Redemption lay at the foundation of the Passover as well as Pentecost. The date of the Passover depended on the ripening of the barley. If the grain failed to mature, the paschal season was delayed a month. Hence Pentecost might also be postponed. In like manner God's timetable of salvation was contingent upon the harvest being ready for the sickle.

The wheat harvest celebrated at Pentecost[10] sprang from a toilsome sowing. During Christ's "life on earth He had sown the seed of truth and had watered it with His blood. The conversions that took place on the Day of Pentecost were the result of this sowing, the harvest of Christ's work, revealing the power of His teaching."[11] The gospel seed, fertilized by the blood of the Paschal Lamb enabled the "first fruits" of Pentecost to be reaped. But had the disciples failed to pray for the Spirit, they would not have received the blessing of Pentecost. "Unless the members of God's church today have a living connection with the Source of all spiritual growth, they will not be ready for the time of reaping. Unless they keep their lamps trimmed and burning, they will fail of receiving added grace in time of special need."[12]

On Friday, the fourteenth of Nisan, Christ died as the true Paschal Lamb. In accordance with the law, the paschal barley sheaf was presented on Sunday the sixteenth. On this day our Lord fulfilled the Old Testament type by rising from the dead as God's antitypical "Wave Sheaf,"[13] or "Firstfruits of them that slept."[14] He was the representative and pledge of the great harvest of souls which one day will be gathered into God's garner. Those whom He raised immediately after His own resurrection, and then took to heaven at His ascension forty days later, were the sample and guarantee of the precious sheaves of earth's final reaping. Jesus had earlier made a remarkable prediction concerning His resurrection. "Except a corn of wheat fall to the ground and die, it abideth alone: but if it die, it bringeth forth much fruit."[15] Rising from the dead, the life-giving wheat brought forth a hundredfold. And on the Day of Pentecost multitudes were presented to God as the two leavened loaves of bread.

From the day of His resurrection the disciples counted fifty days to Pentecost.[16] During the first forty of these Jesus had remained on earth, appearing to individuals and groups, and even addressing five hundred of His followers at one time. Then, in company with His eleven faithful ones, He had climbed the Mount of Olives, and, bidding them tarry in Jerusalem until they had been endued with heavenly power, He ascended to His Father.

For the next ten days, one hundred and twenty believers[17] had prayed for Christ's promised Gift. And then "on the day of Pentecost the Infinite One revealed himself in power to the church. By His Holy Spirit He descended from the heights of heaven as a rushing, mighty wind, to the room in which the disciples were assembled. It was as if for ages this influence had been held in restraint, and now heaven rejoiced in being able to pour upon the church the riches of the Spirit's power. . . . They grasped the imparted gift. And what followed?—Thousands were converted in a day. The sword of the Spirit, newly edged with power, and bathed in the lightnings of heaven, cut its way through unbelief. . . . They were filled with an intense longing . . . to arouse and do their part, that all nations might hear the truth, and the earth be filled with the glory of the Lord."[18]

The occasion for this predicted[19] flood of grace upon the earth was Christ's inauguration as High Priest in the celestial sanctuary. His sacrifice had been accepted by His Father on the resurrection morning, and now, in response to His first mediative act as mankind's representative, Heaven granted unstinted gifts of the Spirit to the members of His church. While Jesus was officially assuming His position as Priest and High Priest among supernal beings, the Spirit was fitting His followers as "kings and priests" to be His ambassadors among sinful men.

When Christ was anointed as man's "advocate with the Father"[20] the apostles were set apart as Christs's evangelists to the highways and hedges of earth. Through His Spirit our Lord thus bound His followers to Himself in "heavenly places" and shared His ministry of reconciliation with them to the end of time. The Pentecostal outpouring was the seal of this union in service and "Heaven's communication that the Redeemer's inauguration was accomplished."[21] The Old Testament church had been instructed and organized at the first Pentecost at Sinai, while the New Testament church was empowered and set in motion for its task at the last Pentecost at Jerusalem.

Through the centuries of Hebrew history each Pentecost should have been a joyous acknowledgment of God's bountiful gifts. Climaxing the grain harvests, it provided an annual opportunity to celebrate and feast on what had been sown in tears and reaped in joy. Unlike the dedication of the unleavened paschal grain, two loaves of leavened bread were presented to the Lord at Pentecost as a thank offering.[22] Fifty days earlier a simple sheaf of barley, natural, and touched by no human hands, had been consecrated. But now at Pentecost, wheat had been reaped, threshed, ground to flour, leavened, salted, kneaded into loaves with water, and baked in an oven.[23] The grains of paschal barley might have themselves been sown to produce one hundredfold, but the grain of the Pentecostal loaves, crushed and cooked, provided bread for hungry souls.

These two loaves,[24] although constituting a meal offering, "required neither oil nor frankincense" and represented man's cooperative efforts coupled with God's gifts. "The leaven for them is not apart from their dough, and with this they are leavened."[25] Leaven is a type of the pervasive influence of an external principle, either good or bad, which works silently from within to transform the substance into which it is introduced. During the paschal octave no leaven was acceptable to God, but during Pentecost these two leavened loaves of wheat flour were specifically required. Could the Saviour have alluded to this in His parable of the woman who took three measures of meal and put leaven into them?[26] "In the twelve disciples the leaven of truth was hidden by the Great Teacher."[27] Was it possible that these two loaves represented Christ's Spirit-begotten, truth-filled church members made up of both Jews and Gentiles, in whom the hidden principles of Christ's life were now working?

The amount of flour in the loaves was double that required at the Passover. The "double portion" might suggest honor or heirship, as illustrated by Elkanah's treatment of his favorite wife,

Hannah[28] and Elijah's legacy to his beloved acolyte Elisha.[29] At Pentecost, Christ "the Heir of all things," accepted gifts from His Father which honored Him, and then shared them with His people by baptizing them with the Spirit to make them "joint heirs with" Him.

The wheat for these loaves was harvested from the best district in Palestine, threshed and ground at the temple, and sieved through twelve sieves to a quality of utmost fineness. This flour was kneaded with lukewarm water and baked the evening prior to the feast. The rabbis remind us that they were four handbreadths wide, and seven handbreadths long, and four fingers high, altogether containing about four pounds of flour.

Besides these two loaves of leavened wheat bread by which Israel fulfilled its national obligations, each family was enjoined to bring a basket of its own wheat harvest to the place of worship.[30] The Lord required His church as a whole, as well as His people individually, to present offerings of gratitude to Him. Accompanying these loaves the law required His people to sacrifice two young bulls, one ram, and seven yearling lambs, with their appropriate meal offerings and libations, as tokens of consecration.[31] One male kid was slain as a sin offering, and two lambs as peace offerings[32] to express national gratitude. And with these offerings of dedication, God's covenant people cemented their relationship with Jehovah.

After "heaving" the two loaves before the altar of perpetual sacrifice, as a gift of gratitude to God, the high priest took one for himself and gave the other to be divided among the priests.[33] Our great High Priest shared His rewards with His "royal priests," and in this way the church on earth was united with the church in heaven,[34] and Jew and Gentile became one.[35]

The Hebrews believed that God gave them His law at Sinai on the first Pentecost. Maimondes long ago said: "Just as one who is expecting the most faithful of his friends is wont to count the days and hours to his arrival, so we also count from the omer of the day of exodus from Egypt to that of the giving of the law, which was the object of the exodus, as it is said: 'I bear you on eagle's wings, and brought you to Myself.' And because this great manifestation did not last more than one day, there we annually commemorate it only one day."[36]

Ellen White corroborates this link. "God had commanded Moses to bring his people to this place of natural solitude and sublimity, that they might hear his voice, and receive the statute book of heaven. Fifty days previous to this the pillar of fire had lighted the path through the Red Sea that God had miraculously opened before the marching multitudes of his people. They had since then made their way slowly onward through the desert."[37] On the last Pentecost in Jerusalem tongues of the same Fire that had illuminated Israel's path lighted the way of true Israel toward the heavenly Canaan.

At Sinai the Hebrew people had received the law "by the hand of a mediator," Moses, who had ascended the mount no fewer than seven times, perhaps suggesting a "perfect" or complete journey. On Zion the church received the Spirit through their celestial Mediator, who had perfected His sacrificial mission and had scaled the heights of the heavenly Zion. On Moses' final return from Sinai, the skin of his face reflected God's glory as a mirror does the sun. He brought with him the revelation of God's will in the decalogue, as well as the plan of salvation displayed in the sanctuary. The first showed the standard of conduct which God expected of mankind; the second described the way of renewal whenever they failed. On the final Pentecost our great Mediator had ascended to His Father, had been accepted as Priest and Sacrifice, and had requested His choicest Gift, the Holy Spirit, for His family on earth. By His power the members of His church may now successfully make their own approach to God. At the first Pentecost Moses, who died, had been glorified as Israel's temporary mediator, while at the last Pentecost, Christ, who ever lives, was glorified as the eternal Mediator.[38]

Luke recorded Peter's insightful statement that Christ had given His Spirit to His disciples in partial fulfillment of Joel's prophecy.[39] But this Gift had been granted only because of the petitions of His faithful followers.[40] Daniel prayed for the release of his people on time;[41] and Anna, Simeon, Nathaniel, and other pious Israelites besought the Lord to send the Messiah speedily.[42] In keeping with this principle,[43] Jesus urged His disciples to continue to pray for the promised Spirit.[44] We should pray for the Spirit at the very time He is due,[45] so that the pressage of

Pentecost may reach its consummation,[46] and the work of the third angel climax.[47]

God designed that worshipers should unite their petitions with the incense ascending from the golden altar. After Aaron had offered sacrifice, and incense had risen in silent intercession, the glory of God filled the tabernacle.[48] Following Solomon's sacrifice and prayer, the light of the Shekinah pervaded the temple.[49] When the Lord promised, "I will put my spirit within you,"[50] He encouraged His people to pray: "I will yet for this be enquired of by the house of Israel, to do it for them."[51] In the upper room, all the disciples were together, all were of one accord, all praying, and then all were filled with the Spirit.[52] Emboldened by these examples, let us pray for the Spirit so that we may celebrate our personal Pentecosts.

Paul compared what happened at Horeb with the experience in the upper room. "If the ministration of death . . . was glorious," he asked, "how shall not the ministration of the spirit be rather glorious?"[53] At Sinai there were accompaniments of thunder and lightening, blare of trumpet, reeling of rocks, and the voice proclaiming God's eternal moral and ceremonial laws.[54]

The ministry of the sanctuary explained at this time was the ministration based on the death of sacrifices. But in Jerusalem, the wind and the sound from heaven which marked the gift of the Spirit[55] directed all to the living Saviour. The voice at Sinai proclaiming the law which defined sin spoke through fire-cleansed[56] lips the gospel which saves from sin.

From Pentecost we watch the pioneers of the fledgling church stride out of old Jerusalem and into the world. Their nationalism was sublimated, their selfishness gone, their racism banished, and the world blotted from their affections. With their love paramount, and their possessions on the altar of humanity's need, the new society of the Nazarene speedily overthrew the citadels of darkness with the unsheathed sword of the Spirit. Pentecost demonstrated that Deity dwelt in human hearts. The words of the disciples testified that the One once crucified was now minstering in of the heavenly sanctuary, and their Spirit-filled lives demonstrated the vitality and power of indwelling grace, while their voices proclaimed, "All our *gifts* are Christ's."

Chapter 10

Feast of Tabernacles

Festival of the Everlasting Father

All my *future* is Christ's

The Feast of Tabernacles was the last, and, at the time of Christ, the most popular of Israel's festivals.[1] It was called *Succoth*, or "The Feast of Booths"[2] because the pilgrims lived in structures made of leaves and branches. "Booth," meaning a lair[3] suggests a simple bucolic hut, while its Greek equivalent[4] has been used for a container,[5] the Mosaic tabernacle,[6] and the wings of the Shekinah.[7] John used the word for Christ's pavilion of love spread over the righteous[8] and rejoiced with David to see the saints dwelling "in the house of the Lord for ever."[9] Israel left Egypt, "the house of bondage," for these shelters from the sun and rain.

These leafy huts were erected on the flat roofs of Jerusalem, in its courtyards and streets, and even within the temple precincts, and spilled over the neighboring hills for the distance of a Sabbath day's journey.[10] Made of the branches of pine, reminder of fragrance; palm, emblem of victory; olive, symbol of fruitfulness; myrtle, token of modesty; and willow, memorial of tears wiped away; they were completed by the fourteenth of Tishri, the seventh month, and occupied from the fifteenth for one week.

During this time Jerusalem "bore the appearance of a beautiful forest,"[11] painted, not with spring's living green, but in the dying reds and golds and browns of autumn. These cascades of leaves touched with decay whispered that man's day would soon end and wrote the epitaph of Israel's pilgrimage. The rustle of the dry leaves rasping out the dirge of a dying order encouraged the people to think of spring's renewing.

84

During the Feast of Unleavened Bread the wave-sheaf of barley had been consecrated, and at Pentecost the two leavened wave-loaves of wheat flour dedicated. And now at the Feast of Ingathering[12] Israel's final harvest from orchard and vineyard were celebrated. "It was God's design that at this time the people should reflect on His goodness and mercy"[13] in providing material blessings.[14] The worshipers assembled at the sanctuary in holiday mood, and their offerings registered their gratitude.[15]

The short, bracing autumn days roused a yearning for nightly warmth and gaiety and invited the people to temple fellowship. Household chores were forgotten, while each evening the pilgrims enjoyed a feast with guests from the needy and lonely—Levites, widows, orphans, and strangers.[16] "Israelites born"[17] dwelling in booths remembered the nomadic lives of Abraham and the patriarchs, as well as the years in the desert, and recalled the fact that in every age God's elect had been pilgrims and strangers on this earth.[18]

"The feast of ingathering, which is in the end of the year"[19] marked not only the culmination of Israel's sacred cycle, but also the commencement of a period of rest and hope. *End* here suggests "going out," as well as "coming in," and may be translated "beginning" and also "ending." It describes the rising sun[20] and the birth of a child.[21] The festive week was a time for introspection into life's cycles.

The solemn rites of the Day of Atonement, five days previous, had driven each worshiper to an examination of his own life; and as Azazel's goat had been led away, it had brought peace to the camp. And then the psalm, "O give thanks unto the Lord, for he is good: for his mercy endureth for ever" had risen in triumph from the pilgrims trudging to the Holy City for the Feast of Tabernacles. The Hebrews called this simply "The Feast,"[22] and Josephus remembered that it was the "most holy and most eminent" of festivals."[23]

To the week of celebrations[24] an eighth day was added,[25] the first and last days being "holy convocations,"[26] the sixth and seventh of the annual ceremonial sabbaths. During the intervening time business might be transacted.[27]

The dedication of the tabernacle[27] and the temples erected by Solomon[28] and Zerubabel[29] occurred at the Feast of Tabernacles, anticipating the time when God would erect His "Tabernacle" among the sons of men[30] by sending "the desire of all nations."[31] But in spite of these inspiring associations, precaptivity Israel seems largely to have neglected it. In the time of Nehemiah the scribe remembered that "since the days of Jeshua the son of Nun unto that day had not the children of Israel" kept such a Feast of Tabernacles.[32]

Overlooked in prosperity, gratitude to God was shown by the handful of captives that returned to a desolated land and a desecrated temple. Those who had hung their harps on the willows of Chaldea to weep made booths of the willows of Canaan to rejoice. This grateful remnant came back joyously to God's harvest home, to exchange the mattock of servitude for the palm branch of salvation, and booths were again built amid the rubble of the Holy City.

Each day, from the sixteenth to the twentieth of Tishri, later called "the middle of the week,"[33] and especially during the sabbatic year, the law was taught to the assembled multitudes.[34] Ezra himself read the law "day by day, from the first day unto the last."[35] During His final Feast of Tabernacles, Jesus called attention to this practice by asking, "Did not Moses give you the law, and yet none of you keepeth the law?"[36]

Besides the regular morning and evening offerings, 199 sacrifices peculiar to this celebration were presented. These were gradually diminished from thirty animals on the first day, to one bull, one ram, one kid, and seven lambs slaughtered on the final day.[37] These diminishing victims looked to the time when all offerings will merge into the one great living Sacrifice.[38]

At the time of the morning sacrifice each day, a priest with a golden pitcher led a joyous procession of worshipers and a choir of Levites to the Pool of Siloam.[39] Filling his vessel from this Spring of Peace, he raised it to his shoulder and turned toward the temple. This was the signal for all who were near enough to drink at the pool. The observers on the slopes of Zion and Olivet then burst into jubilant praise: "The Lord Jehovah is my strength and my song; . . . with joy shall ye draw water out of the wells of salvation."[40]

The priest carrying the water trudged up to the temple, pausing every ten paces while trumpets pealed and Levites sang. As the concourse swept into the temple by the Water Gate, every worshiper joined in the psalm, "Our feet shall stand within thy gates, O Jerusalem."[41] The water presented at the altar gave rise to the expression "House of Outpouring."[42]

This rite celebrated the water which God had supplied to His people from the riven rock[43] and looked toward the grace of the Messiah, the pierced Rock.[44] Shiloh was Jacob's prophetic name for Christ,[45] and the drawing of water from the Pool of Siloam, also meaning "Sent,"[46] was both commemorative and predictive. To the thoughtful worshiper "the water flowing from the smitten rock was associated with the outpouring of the Holy Spirit, which they expected to receive when the Messiah should come."[47]

"When in a golden vessel the waters of Siloam were borne by the priests into the temple, and, after being mingled with wine, were poured over the sacrifice on the altar, there was great rejoicing. A multitude of voices, mingled with the sound of the trumpet and the cymbal, united in ascribing praise to the most high God."[48]

During the festivities "above all the confusion of the crowd and the shouts of rejoicing, a voice is heard: 'If any man thirst, let him come unto me, and drink.' The attention of the people is arrested. Outwardly all is joy; but the eye of Jesus, beholding the throng with the tenderest compassion, sees the soul, parched, and thirsting for the waters of life. And yet many who were eagerly seeking to satisfy the wants of the soul by a round of empty ceremonies, to quench their thirst from cisterns that hold no water, understood not their great need. They manifested great outward joy that the fountain had been opened, but they refused to drink of its life-giving waters themselves. Today "the fountain of life has been opened for us." "It is our privilege and duty to drink."[49]

Near the altar were "two silver basins, with a priest standing at each one. The flagon of water was poured into one, and a flagon of wine into the other; and the contents of both flowed into a pipe which communicated with the Kedron, and was conducted to the Dead Sea."[50] Wine symbolized the blood of Jesus which ratified the new covenant,[51] while water typified the cleansing provided by the incarnate and inspired Word.[52] This ritual portrayed the merits of the Great Sacrifice bubbling into the sterile world of death from the sanctuary,[53] and wherever it flowed those dead in their sins were restored to life.[54]

This ceremony signaled for every worshiper to rejoice. So intense was this that the Jews recollect that "he that never saw the rejoicing of drawing water, never saw rejoicing in all his life."[55] Before Canaan had been settled, the Lord had commanded, "Thou shalt rejoice in thy feast,"[56] and so each evening the celebrants repaired to the temple to participate, or found places on the hills around the city from which to observe. "The court was a scene of great rejoicing. Gray-haired men, the priests of the temple and the rulers of the people, united in the festive dances to the sound of instrumental music and the chants of the Levites."[57]

Each man carried in his right hand a frond of palm and three sprigs of myrtle tied together with one of willow as an emblem of triumph,[58] while in his left had he held a branch of citrus with its fruit.[59] This bouquet was called a *Lulab*.[60] All who were able marched around the altar waving these signs of plenty. On the seventh day they marched around it seven times to commemorate the destruction of Jericho.[61] Psalms were sung,[62] and everyone was glad that God had given Israel victory over their sins.[63] On the twenty-first of Tishri the booths were dismantled and burned, the children ate the oranges or other citrus fruit, and the people prepared to return home.

During this day, called the Great Hosanna, the people waved their *Lulabs*, singing, "Hosanna for Thy sake, O our Creator; Hosanna for Thy sake, O our Redeemer; Hosanna for Thy sake, O our Seeker; Hosanna!" as if unwittingly invoking the Trinity.[64] In the hosannas and waving palm branches of Christ's triumphal entry into Jerusalem the people felt the Messianic fulfillment of these ceremonies.[65]

At sundown each evening lamps were lighted in the temple courts. Unnecessary while the Shekinah had appeared, the leaders of Israel instituted this ceremony after the captivity. During Christ's time two lofty standards, supporting lampstands of great size,[66] were placed in the court, and many other lamps located in different parts of the sacred area. These shallow earthen dishes contained wicks suffused with oil. Following the evening sacrifice a spark from the altar was touched to these lamps, and the "temple and its court blazed with artificial light."[67] This illumination commemorated "the pillar of light that guided Israel in the desert, and was also regarded as pointing to the coming of the Messiah."[68]

"In the illumination of Jerusalem, the people expressed their hope of the Messiah's coming to shed His light upon Israel. But to Jesus the scene had a wider meaning. As the radiant lamps of the temple lighted up all about them, so Christ, the source of spiritual light, illumines the darkness of the world. Yet the symbol was imperfect. That great light which His own hand had set in the heavens was a truer representation of the glory of His mission."[69] Our Lord desired that this temple should serve the needs of all nations[70] and purposed that, like the sun, His truth should illumine "every man that cometh into the world."[71] Isaiah foretold that the light of the Messiah would dispel the exclusiveness of the Jews,[72] and it was during the Feast of Tabernacles[73] that Jesus claimed to be the Light of the world,[74] the fulfillment of these predictions.

Light is a symbol of God Himself. Light created life when dark waters flooded the deep[75] and in the camp of Hebron marched along the blood-drenched way to covenant with the father of the faithful.[76] Light revealed the incarnation through the glowing shrub of Horeb[77] and guided a rabble to conquer Canaan.[78] Light came to Sinai to legislate[79] and vindicated the faith of Elijah on Carmel's desecrated heights.[80] And when the Cradle bridged the chasm caused by sin, light encircled the manger and shone into the trustful minds of shepherds in the fields of Bethlehem.[81] And so Christ's claim to be "the light of the world" brought insight to those with "ears to hear."

Light had yet to rout the hosts of darkness about His tomb and proclaim the ending of the night of death.[82] Light was to anoint the stammering lips of the disciples in an unknown upper room and freight them with the saving story of a risen Saviour.[83] Light was to free Peter,[84] convert Saul,[85] comfort Paul,[86] and illumine the beloved disciple in the cave of Revelation,[87] and thence fling radiance into the darkest corners of the earth, and finally focus on the face of the returning Prince of Peace.

While the lamps were being lighted, Levite choirs, stationed on the fifteen steps which corresponded to the fifteen "Psalms of

Degrees" (Psalms 120-134), sang them to the accompaniment of musical instruments. To the worshipers rejoicing in the light of the blazing lamps of the temple came memories of the past glories of their nation and hopes of future blessing. The Christian pilgrim need no longer journey to the Holy City, for the Light of the world is glowing along his path. And because Jesus died, the fountain is flowing, and His blood-ratified covenant is ready to bring victory into every life.

The eighth day, the twenty-second of Tishri, "the great day of the feast," rounded out the festive season and was observed as a sabbath rest and a holy convocation. The people no longer lived in booths, the pouring of the water was suspended, and the lamps had flickered out. For the year the Feast of Tabernacles was over, but its purpose continued. It "not only pointed back to the wilderness sojourn, but, as the feast of harvest, it . . . pointed forward to the great day of final ingathering, when the Lord of harvest shall send forth His reapers to gather the tares together in bundles for the fire, and to gather the wheat into His garner."[88]

The seer observed that in the earth made new "it shall come to pass, that every one that is left of all the nations . . . shall even go up from year to year to worship the King . . . and to keep the feast of tabernacles."[89] And this prediction is soon to be fulfilled; for "in this mountain shall the Lord of hosts make unto all people a feast of fat things, a feast of wines . . . on the lees . . . well refined. . . . He will swallow up death in victory; and the Lord God will wipe away tears from off all faces."[90]

On that day the ransomed hosts will journey across the recreated earth to the Feast of the Father's Harvest Home. They will dwell with Him in the New Jerusalem, not in temporary huts of leaves tinged with decay, but in the mansions made especially for them,[91] rejoicing, not in the flickering light of lamps of clay with wicks of flax, soon to be consumed, but in the serene radiance of the Lamb, the eternal Light of that place.[92] And there they will drink satisfying draughts, not from the spring of Siloam, breaking from the dark bosom of the unfeeling rock, but from the ever-flowing river of life, eternally springing from the heart of God.[93] To them the Father calls, "Come, ye blessed," and they joyously respond, "all our *future* is Christ's."

Chapter 11
Sabbath of Years and Jubilee
All my *freedom* is Christ's

Amid the thunders of Sinai the Lord legislated two unique celebrations in the religious, economic, agricultural, and social calendar of the Hebrews.[1] Every seventh year was to be spent sabbatically, while the fiftieth was to be observed as the Jubilee.

The epithets applied to the sabbatic year are instructive. Called "the seventh year,"[2] "the release" or "the year of release,"[3] it gave opportunity for debts to be canceled and bondmen freed. Designated "a sabbath of rest" or "rest of entire rest,"[4] as well as "a year of rest unto the Land,"[5] it required cessation of all agricultural work. As "the sabbath of the land,"[6] it reminded God's people to leave their fields fallow to rebuild the soil. Termed "a sabbath to the Lord,"[7] it provided leisure to worship the Creator and study His works. The expression "the Lord's release"[8] pointed to Him whose love cancels indebtedness, and grants freedom from servitude.

The sabbatic year commenced after the harvest of the sixth year had been garnered,[9] probably during the Feast of Tabernacles. However, should the rule for starting the Jubilee apply, the sabbatic year would begin at the call of the trumpet at the close of the Day of Atonement[10] which fell in the sixth year, as the Jubilee did in the forty-ninth year. Because it followed seven complete "weeks of years," the Jubilee might well be termed the Pentecost of Years.

The conquest of Canaan under Joshua took six years,[11] and after this arduous conflict the sabbatic year provided Israel with a well-earned rest. During it they recalled the blessings which the Lord had bestowed and the promises He had fulfilled.

Like the Sabbath commandment, the law governing the sabbatic year opened with an injunction to labor.[12] The Israelites were to work their fields and vineyards for six years before resting during the seventh.

While wandering in the wilderness they had shown their faith and obedience by gathering on the sixth, or preparation day, a "double portion" of manna to meet their needs for the seventh.[13] In the Holy Land God required them to demonstrate their submission by setting aside enough food during the preparation year for the sabbatic year,[14] promising that His blessing would reward their faithfulness.[15] The organization needed in husbanding the produce of field and orchard trained His people to plan carefully and to trust God implicitly.

During these two years the Lord required a cessation of agriculture.[16] What the Sabbath was to people, the sabbatic year was to be to the land. Farmers were forbidden to till or sow their fields or prune their vineyards and orchards, nor were the spontaneous products of the ground to be harvested by its owner. All that the earth produced was to be considered communal property.[17] The landowner was to exercise no more claim to the bounties of his acres than might the poorest vagrant, nor must he use his rights to chase away any who gathered the produce of his property.[18] Even beasts and birds were not to be scared off, for God remembered their harried little lives.[19]

In these ways the Lord taught His people that what they claimed as their land, was actually His,[20] and that its yield was theirs on lease, to be shared at His request for the enjoyment of every creature. In fact, in no year might the owner reap the entire harvest of his fields.[21] Through these regulations He wished to enhance the value that His people placed upon the quality of the lives of their fellows, as well as on those of the lesser creatures. The Creator cares for all living things, and His stewards must reflect His sentiments. The sabbatic year and the Jubilee taught principles of divine ecological management.

Since no pruning was permitted, orchards and vineyards were left "undressed,"[22] a word which describes the Nazarite whose undressed hair[23] testified to his consecration to God. The Lord intended that as neighboring nations observed the shaggy and uncultivated fields, they would recognize this as a sign of Israel's obedience to Jehovah. But, unlike faithful Nazarites,[24] Hebrew landowners have left no record of their observance of the sabbatic year or Jubilee prior to their return from Babylonian captivity. Instead, we read only of their complaint, "What shall we eat?"[25] and note their refusal to obey their Landlord. Because Israel's witness to the world through this divine technique was mute, the Lord allowed their deportation to Assyria and Babylon.[26] Then for seven decades Palestine's fallow land and neglected orchards testified to the dire results of the people's disobedience and the sovereignty of God.[27] Long before this, however, prophets had sounded warnings, and, when the banishment finally occurred, sadly noted this fact.[28]

After the dispossessed land had enjoyed its "sabbath" for seventy years, the returned captives were much more ready to observe these regulations.[29] Josephus recorded the celebration of the Sabbath of Years by the Hebrews as well as the Samaritans.[30] But this compliance was only half-hearted; acceptance of these kindly principles of stewardship, and the generous behavior they required, were missing.

The Lord promised that "the sabbath of the land shall be meat for you."[31] What a paradox! Leisure produce abundance? Forbidden to reap and ordered to leave the land fallow every seventh year, and then for two years each half century, how could the Hebrews ever survive if also required to support resident foreigners as well as beasts and birds? But the Lord guaranteed to supply all they needed and promised that they would be able to pay their vacationing servants on time.[32] His prospering grace would teach them that "man doth not live by bread only."[33] Their bountiful harvests during six years would more than meet their needs for years after the sabbatic year and the Jubilee,[34] while acceptance of His assurance would engender faith and strengthen their characters.

Called the "sabbath of the land,"[35] the sabbatic year taught that as man enjoyed his weekly rest, the land was to "enjoy" its rest also.[36] Intriguing language! Can soil "enjoy" the months it lay fallow? Can land keep sabbath? As man rested on the Sabbath, his physical, mental, and spiritual systems were refreshed and divinely prepared for the toil of the coming week, so the elements of the earth, refreshed and vitalized by God's blessing during the year of sabbatic disuse, received payment for the debt owed to it by those who reaped its harvests, and would then produce richer crops.

Throughout the sabbatic years and Jubilees, "strangers," or foreigners dwelling in Israel, were to be treated with special kindness.[37] These persons had no rights to property or its produce, because the Lord had parceled out the land among the twelve tribes. But God remembered them and reminded His representatives to keep fresh in memory that they had once been the dispossessed minority[38] and to treat others as they would have wished to be cared for. In this way He sought to discipline His people to go the second mile in exercising kindness at regular intervals throughout their lives and to encourage the poor to get out and gather the bounties He provided.

Jehovah assured His people of prosperity on condition of their obedience to His rules regulating their business.[39] "Every seven years thou shalt make a release,"[40] He decreed. The singular *thou* stresses individual responsibility. No one was to incur indebtedness which he could not liquidate in six years.[41] Jacob's three contracts with Laban illustrate this.[42] Should he be unable to repay his obligations after making every effort within this time limit, the debtor was to be released. God's plan guaranteed "no poor among" the obedient.[43] What a prospect! Poverty banished, not by hoarding or by taxing or social insurance, but by brother lending to brother, and by even canceling debts. The wise man observed the effect of the opposite conduct. "There is that [which] withholdeth more than is meet, but it tendeth to poverty."[44] In spite of this wise counsel the Lord sighed that the poor would always exist.[45]

But to curb this avaricious spirit, He warned against refusing to lend the needy because of the proximity of the sabbatic year of Jubilee,[46] and reasoning, Next year is the release, so I will not lend! He promised His cooperation in the business ventures of those who showed this generous and sympathetic attitude. "For this thing the Lord thy God shall bless thee in all thy works, and in all that thou puttest thine hand unto."[47]

The law stipulated that Hebrew slaves, or indentured servants, should be freed after six years of servitude, or in the "year of release."[48] Those who were set free should not go empty-handed, but should be generously furnished with staples to start a new life.[49] But any servant who chose to might remain in the service of his master whom he had grown to love. In fact, God provided a legal ceremony to cement this relationship.[50] But in the Jubilee, even those Hebrews who had received this mark of voluntary servitude were to be emancipated with their entire families. At this time all foreign slaves were also to be set free.[51]

Jehovah assured Israel that by complying with His requirements they would be guaranteed the land in perpetuity. He even assured them that He would keep off all kinds of adversaries,[52] adding, "And if ye shall say, What shall we eat the seventh year? behold, we shall not sow, nor gather in our increase: then I will command my blessing upon you in the sixth year, and it shall bring forth fruit for three years. And ye shall sow the eighth year, and eat yet of old fruit until the ninth year; until her fruits come in ye shall eat of the old store."[53]

Since these years of rest commenced after the harvests had been garnered, the people were surrounded by signs of abundance. God designed that their faith should rest on the evidence of what He had done for them. Paul remarked that "faith cometh by hearing,"[54] but in Israel's case it grew out of seeing and tasting as well!

The Lord provided His people with leisure to rejoice in His goodness and sustaining power and to fellowship with family and friends. He recommended that they should spend this time studying His law, especially during the Feast of Tabernacles. His guidance in the past was to be taught to the children who had "not known any thing" of the experiences of their forebears, so that they might "hear, and learn to fear the Lord your God, as long as ye live in the land whither ye go over Jordan to possess it."[55] Old and young were to use this opportunity to meet their spiritual, social, and physical needs.

The Lord wished His people to realize that food, money, and land were theirs in trust. When He suspended their privileges as tenants for a year or two, He displayed His ownership and disciplined them in true economics.

These years of release and leisure prefigured the "rest" which Christ would bestow on all who learn of Him,[56] and whose "rest shall be glorious."[57] During these times there was no reason not to praise God. The rejoicing servant emancipated from his master, the maid freed by her mistress, the undisturbed beast and bird, and the stranger at home in God's green fields united in worshiping their benevolent Father. The storehouses bulging with provender for several years testified of His blessings. And as Israel studied the law governing the sabbatic year and Jubilee, the link between spiritual power and economic well-being would grow more apparent.

And the Lord promised that obedience to them would pave the way to national greatness and international power. Israel's influence would spread to all nations, with no need to borrow. Protected and prosperous as a community, their way of life would develop into a clear witness to God's love and His beneficent laws,[58] testifying that the earth belonged to Heaven which gave "meat in due season" to every creature.[59] Obedience and stewardship, forgiveness and tolerance, were taught by the rules governing these years of benevolence, and today their message is reflected from the ministry of Him who came to redeem and focuses upon Him who will soon come to restore, and whose servants will serve Him in His land made new where no one will hoard his own, and where the law of love will be paramount and God's will supreme.

Jubile, as the King James Version spells it, is a transliteration of the Hebrew for ram, *yobel* or *jubel*, ram's horn.[60] Scripture designated the fiftieth year as the "Year of the Ram's Horn," or "Release," as the Septuagint explained it. Ezekiel called it the "Year of Liberty."[61] The *jubel* which announced this year was similar to the instruments used in the overthrow of Jericho, where they sounded the opening of the way into the Promised Land. Every fifty years the ram's horn was to announce the commencement of a new epoch or Jubilee.

The time for the beginning of the Jubilee was significant. The Day of Atonement had settled the destiny of each Israelite. When he heard the "joyful sound"[62] of the high priest's golden bells and listened to the assurance of his benediction and the blare of the ram's horn,[63] he joyously added the call of his own *jubel* to the symphony of freedom, and soon every valley and mountain echoed with this signal of universal hope. The Jubilee had overtones of eschatology, anticipating the great emancipation which will follow the world-wide proclamation of the gospel trumpet at the consummation of the antitypical day of atonement.[64] Its very name has given rise to the English word *jubilation*, which means "singing" from an overflowing heart.[65]

The timing of the Jubilee was contingent on the sabbatic year. After the lapse of seven of these heptads, "the fiftieth year"[66] was to be celebrated. Some chronologers choose to think of the forty-ninth year as the Jubilee, to fit their scheme of things. But this contradicts both the Bible designation of the fiftieth year, and the Lord's promise to bless their food supply for three years!

Three special activities characterized the Jubilee. Voluntary Hebrew slaves who had not accepted liberty in the sabbatic year were now set free, and all debts were canceled. But what specially distinguished the Jubilee was the reversion of all landed property to the family or heirs of the original possessor.[67] When forced to leave his home, the debtor must have counted the years to the Jubilee and on its arrival happily repossessed his inheritance.

These regulations were socially revolutionary, and through them the Lord showed His concern for the unfortunates who have "as much right to a place in God's world as have the more wealthy."[68] The Jubilee was a prophetic type of the restoration of the earth made new to its original Landlord and His tenants.

When the heavenly High Priest has completed His intercession on the antitypical day of atonement and returns to earth, He will proclaim the Jubilee and extend His invitation to the disenfranchised, "Come, ye blessed of my Father, inherit."[69] As the second Adam and the Kinsman Redeemer of the human race, He will share His re-created heritage with His family, "justified by his grace . . . [and] heirs according to the hope of eternal life,"[70] born again "to an inheritance incorruptible, and undefiled, and that fadeth not away, reserved in heaven for" them.[71]

Ellen White describes this glorious scene thus: "Jesus' silver trumpet sounded, as He descended on the cloud, wrapped in flames of fire . . . and cried, 'Awake! awake!' . . . The dead came up clothed with immortality."[72] "Then commenced the jubilee, when the land should rest. I saw the pious slave rise in triumph and victory and shake off the chains that bound him."[73] Our High Priest marks "the times of restitution of all things"[74] with

His exultant shout, "The year of My redeemed has come!"[75] as the new earth becomes the home of the saved.

By these benign regulations the Lord sought to check inordinate love of property and the power of monopoly stemming from it. He tried to banish the disdain of the rich who often regard paupers as inferior, and the desperation of the poor which gives rise to the hatred of the rich in a disorganized society.[76] These rules "were designed to bless the rich no less than the poor. They would restrain avarice and a disposition for self-exaltation, and would cultivate a noble spirit of benevolence; and by fostering good will and confidence between all classes, they would promote social order, the stability of government. We are all woven together in the great web of humanity, and whatever we can do to benefit and uplift others will reflect in blessing upon ourselves."

"If the law given by God for the benefit of the poor had continued to be carried out, how different would be the present condition of the world, morally, spiritually, and temporally! Selfishness and self-importance would not be manifested as now, but each would cherish a kind regard for the happiness and welfare of others; and such widespread destitution as is now seen in many lands, would not exist. . . . While they might hinder the amassing of great wealth and the indulgence of unbounded luxury, they would prevent the consequent ignorance and degradation of tens of thousands whose ill-paid servitude is required to build up these colossal fortunes. They would bring a peaceful solution of those problems that now threaten to fill the world with anarchy and bloodshed."[77]

Biblical students have wistfully looked forward to the millennium[78] as the fulfillment of the sabbatic year which climaxes some six thousand years of human toil. The untilled and uninhabited planet will then observe its neglected rest. Following this "millennial sabbath" the eternal Jubilee will be celebrated in "the new heavens and the new earth," peopled by the millions emancipated by the Saviour from Satan's servitude, every one at peace, "under the vine and under the fig tree,"[79] subjects of the kingdom intended for them from the beginning by their benevolent Father, singing, "All our *freedom* is Christ's."

Part IV

Defilement

Preview

Sin produces guilt as well as defilement, and in the ritual law this uncleanness is a type of sin. The Scriptures speak of three kinds of sin/uncleanness. Let us review them briefly.

The guilt of sin is revealed by the law, and the opening chapters of Leviticus deal with ceremonies for its removal. Man's moral nature rebels against God's law or falls short of its ideals, and sin results. The sacrificial regulations urged the sinner to confess his sin and transfer his guilt to his substitute victim or to the priest. By these symbolic rites the records of these confessed and forgiven sins, and the guilt resulting from them, were transferred to the sanctuary. The services of the Day of Atonement then covered the final removal of all these evidences of sin.

The uncleanness of sin is connected with bodily "issues" which are concerned with the beginning and ending of life, as well as various products of man's physical being; these also defiled. These exuding toxins were regarded as displaying inner corruption, and contact with them rendered the person "unclean." Leprosy was the classical example of this kind of defiling issue. In Scripture the leper was one whose bodily condition was so dangerous that he must be excluded from society. The very air was tainted with his breath, since his power to defile flowed from within him. The Israelites regarded such a one as dead, and considered that he pictured a person "dead" in his sins.

The third class of sin/uncleanness had to do with the contagion of sin. It resulted from personal contact with a corpse, a bone, or any part of a dead body. This type illustrated the corrosive influence of one who was "dead" in a life of evil conduct. By his words and actions such a person conveyed the virus of his foul example and evil philosophy to any who remained too close to him for too long. (Numbers 19 covers the removal of this.)

Chapter 12

Two Sparrows and the "Issues" of Sin

All my *cleanliness* is Christ's

The dying leper hardly dared to hope that Jesus could help him. He knew he was "full" of the disease, for "its deadly poison permeated his whole body."[1] He had been mourned as worse than dead by family and friends, and besides, no leper had been cleansed in living memory. Why hope? he mused. At last, thrusting aside the sanctions of the law, he had flung himself at Jesus' feet, crying, "Lord, if thou wilt, thou canst make me clean."

Touching his loathsome flesh Christ replied, "I will: be thou clean."[2] "Jesus had no sooner spoken the words of life-giving power, than the half-dead body of putrefaction was changed to healthy flesh, sensitive nerves, and firm muscle."[3] The Lord then bade the jubilant man, "Go, shew thyself to the priest, and offer for thy cleansing, according as Moses commanded." These Levitical regulations we shall now study.[4] Though biblical students are uncertain of the precise malady intended by the law, we shall think of the leprosy there mentioned as including the disease we know, and consider it illustrative of the entire class.

Leprosy was the most dreaded of ancient diseases.[5] Herodotus suspected that it had originated in Egypt. "Egypt" adds focus to Jehovah's promise, "If thou wilt . . . do that which is right . . . I will put none of these diseases upon thee, which I have brought upon the Egyptians."[6]

Leprosy develops in two stages, nodular and anesthetic.[7] At first the skin, stretched over rounded, firm cysts, presents a shiny surface. The sluggish blood pales the complexion until it appears as "white as snow," while underneath rottenness lurks. Becoming reddish brown, the nodules eventually ulcerate into "raw flesh," and the surface nerves slowly cease to register pain. This results in leprosy's anesthetic stage. Weakness and paralysis occur, and because he feels no hurt, the leper grows careless, allowing his extremities to be broken open by striking sharp objects. These wounds ulcerate, suppurating toxic "issues."

The leper's mucus membrane and respiratory tract become affected, while his voice coarsens, and by Hebrew law, must be raised in mournful warnings, "Unclean! Unclean!" His hair grows yellow or gray and drops out. His bones soften, while his hard palate atrophies. Unable to masticate, malnutrition hastens his end.

"Deep-rooted, ineradicable, deadly, it was looked upon as a symbol of sin. By the ritual law the leper was pronounced unclean. Whatever he touched was unclean. The air was polluted by his breath. Like one already dead, he was shut out from the habitation of men. . . . Away from his friends and kindred the leper must bear the curse of his malady."[8] Leprosy thus presented a gruesome picture of what man is by nature, corroded by his inner sinfulness, and exuding evil.

Because the Jews considered leprosy a judgment from God, they termed it "the stroke."[9] Isaiah described the Messiah as "stricken," an expression used of a leper. Based on this, the Talmud called Him "the leper of the house of Judah." Jerome, Aquilla, and Symmachus translated the prophet's phrase, "stricken with leprosy." Jesus did indeed assume man's leprous condition symbolically, and sinless, bore his loathsome curse.

Moses needed insight into his own character, so Yahweh requested that he place his hand on his heart.[10] In biblical sign language "hand" represents man's daily work,[11] and "heart" the seat of his inner dynamics. Withdrawing it, Moses saw in horror that his hand had become leprous. This acted parable revealed to Israel's future leader the quality of his inner motives.

Miriam grew envious of Ziporah, the Midianite wife of Moses[12] and railed against her sister-in-law. For her vindictive slander of the private life of the Hebrew lawgiver she was struck with leprosy. "The judgment visited upon Miriam should be a rebuke to all who yield to jealousy, and murmur against those upon whom God lays the burden of His work."[13] Backbiting and envy are as deadly as leprosy.

Gehazi might have become Elisha's successor, but years of association with the man of God failed to benefit his character. His lying to Naaman and attempts to mislead the prophet revealed covetousness and defiance against God's law. He was ready to sell his integrity for a dream of grandeur and two suits of clothes.[14] "For the deception practiced by Gehazi there could be pleaded no excuse. To the day of his death he remained a leper, cursed of God and shunned by his fellow men."[15] Avarice and materialism are as corrupting as leprosy.

Uzziah was one of Judah's great kings. When "he did that which was right in the sight of the Lord, . . . God made him to prosper." Then Inspiration wistfully added, "He was marvelously helped, till he was strong. But when he was strong, his heart was lifted up to his destruction: for he . . . went into the temple of the Lord to burn incense."[16]

God had stipulated that only priests might perform this rite and had demonstrated the importance of His rule during the rebellion of Korah, Dathan, and Abiram, and the two hundred and fifty princes. Asserting that the laity now had equal rights, the king arrogantly brushed aside the remonstrances of Azariah the high priest and persisted in his rashness until halted by God. "The sin that resulted so disastrously to Uzziah was one of presumption. . . . While standing there, in wrathful rebellion, he was suddenly smitten with a divine judgment. Leprosy appeared on his forehead."[17] High-handed attempts to do what the Lord has not sanctioned are as corrosive as leprosy.

The Levitical law identified three areas in which leprosy appears: (1) human flesh,[18] (2) decaying garments,[19] and (3) corroded houses.[20] Each symbolic category is eloquent with gospel truth. The Levitical regulations provide clues by which these conditions may be identified in life's experiences and then give methods for dealing with each of them.

Leprosy in the body depicts sinful human nature and is God's hieroglyph for the corrupt and corrupting heart.[21] The suspected person was to be quarantined and observed for twice "seven days." Should his condition remain unchanged, the priest was to pronounce him clean. But if the affliction progressed, he was declared unclean, and driven from the camp. Two illustrations show the stringency with which this rule was enforced: the four unfortunate lepers obliged to remain outside Samaria even during a siege,[22] and king Uzziah banished from his capitol, notwithstanding his wealth and power.[23] The leper must live alone in "a house of emancipation,"[24] regarded as legally dead, and therefore free from civil and familial responsibilities.

Leprosy of garments rustles with evil and seductive outward conduct. Adam and Eve sewed aprons, the first clothes ever designed by man, to conceal their nakedness, only to display the truth that man's best efforts to hide his guilty self are but fig-leaf equivalents of "filthy rags." Leprosy in garments was probably caused by various molds. Hugh Macmillan noted a century ago that these fungi are "ubiquitous, and grow as readily on clothing as on house walls, when left in damp, ill-ventilated, ill-lighted places. The reddish patches, however," he continued, "seem to me to have been produced by the growth of the *sporendonema*, or red mold, very common on cheese; or of the *palmella prodigiosa*. This last mentioned plant is occasionally found . . . extending itself over a considerable area. It is usually a gelatinous mass with the color and general appearance of coagulated blood, whence it has received the famous name of gory-dew."[25]

Leprosy of garments typifies self-made cloaks of good deeds and benign feelings besmirched with ingrained and poisonous streaks of uncleanness. The Levitical law provided no hope for such leprous clothing; it must be stripped off and destroyed. Only Christ's righteousness, a robe woven on the loom of heaven,[26] without speck of decay or stain of sin, can adequately clothe the penitent. And today the heavenly Merchantman urges all to buy these "fine linen" garments without money.[27]

Leprosy in dwellings weeps of defiled and disintegrating homes. The law allowed such buildings to be scraped and refurbished. But "if a house gave evidence of conditions that rendered it unsafe for habitation, it was destroyed."[28] The condition of leprosy in homes was also brought about by fungi. These spread in the walls as veins packed closely together, often appearing orange or reddish brown. When mature they distill drops of water, giving rise to the sobriquet *lacrymans*, weeping. The green and red streaks noted in the law were probably caused by another fungus, *murullus lacrymans*, similar to green mold or *penicillium glaucum*. When they ripen they produce millions of minute spores, which, when airborne to suitable sites, establish themselves with incredible speed. When a house was suspected of this dry rot the law called for a period of quarantine, with doors and windows closed, conditions needed for such molds to luxuriate. If the priest then concluded that the dwelling was infested, he ordered the offending plaster and stones to be scraped away, and the walls rebuilt. Thereafter, should the dry rot reappear, the building was condemned.

The Lord warned that He might Himself "put the plague of leprosy in a house"[29] in the Promised Land. This "stroke" He sent in mercy, to give the householder evidence of the hidden, insidious uncleanliness of his home, and to urge him to seek immediate remedies. The Targum of Jonathan renders this: "And if there be a man who buildeth his house with stolen goods [perhaps a stolen wife] . . . than I will put . . ." When the priest pronounced the house clean, the blood of a sparrow was sprinkled on its door posts. The rabbis remember that homes within the walls of Zion, however, never developed leprosy.[30] Take courage, Church of God!

Inspiration describes leprosy as being "cleansed," rather than healed, and evidently considered it a symbol of defilement more than a disease, and so sent the leper, not to the physician, but to the priest. All the minister could do, however, was to pronounce the unfortunate unclean. Does this illustrate the truth of the Father's committing all judgment to His Son?[31] And Jesus was also the Great Physician.

But let us return to our leper. Obeying the Saviour's command, he immediately set out for the temple. Rabbinic tradition had long affirmed that the Messiah would cleanse lepers. For the eight centuries following Naaman's cleansing, there is no record of such an occurrence, and by the time of Christ the priests must have considered the laws dealing with restored lepers obsolete. Jesus deliberately sent these persons to the temple to apprise these functionaries of the fact that the Messiah had indeed come.[32] The first cleansed leper asking for his ritual restoration must have driven the priests to the book of Leviticus, their manual of instruction!

The law first emphasized the thoroughness with which the examination of the leper should be carried out. The priest was not to investigate on the Sabbath, in inadequate light, or to pronounce upon the leper's kindred. Should his sight be defective, he was prohibited from ruling at all! The suspected person was granted every advantage, for any "doubt in leprosy signs, in the beginning, is regarded as clean," but "when uncleanness is established, a condition of doubt is regarded as unclean."[33] Since the Lord ordered only His ministers to adjudicate, no Israelite was to express opinions or to act as a talebearer. The Giver of these regulations has also entrusted His New Testament church leaders with responsibilities to "open" and "shut" and "bind" and "loose."[34]

Isaiah compared sinners to lepers. "Why should ye be stricken?" he asked Israel, using a term for the infliction of leprosy.[35] The prophet predicted that this condition would also be found in the church.[36] But no one need remain in this state, for the gospel provides immediate cleansing. Jesus did not at once grant some requests for healing. For instance, during the illness of Lazarus he waited some days.[37] But when a leper appealed to Him, He responded quickly, and thus called attention to His readiness to cleanse from sin.

When the leper was ready for rehabilitation, the priest was to go out of the camp to find him, thus representing our heavenly Priest's leaving His Father's home to search out sinners. When the leper whom Jesus cleansed requested restoration, he discovered that the priest who had pronounced him unclean years before was on duty. The Lord had warned him not to disclose the identity of the One who had cleansed him, lest prejudice warp his decision.[38] "Who is he that condemneth? It is Christ that died,"[39] our Judge as well as our Priest.

Having established that the leper was free from all symptoms, the priest explained to the happy man how his ritual reinstatement was to be carried out. He must provide two sparrows, a cedar stick, a length of red string, three sprigs of hyssop,[40] a new earthenware jar, a little olive oil, three lambs, and the makings of meal and wine offerings.[41] The same requirements were prescribed for a king as for a slave, for all sinners are equal in God's sight. Let us study each of these items as they focus on aspects of the Saviour's character and ministry.

Sparrows were perhaps the most common of Palestinian birds.

While some doubt whether the leper's sacrifice was actually a sparrow, the Hebrew name, an onomatopoeic word meaning "a twitterer," together with its Assyrian cognate *saparu*, has led to the conclusion that the birds were probably sparrows, as the margin of the King James Version suggests.[42] While not domesticated, sparrows live close to people, even building their nests under the eaves of human habitations, and eating the crumbs which fall from their tables. They were esteemed of little value,[43] and in Christ's time, when the market for sparrows used in the cleansing ceremonies of lepers was opening after 800 years, five of them might be purchased for two farthings,[44] the least valuable of coins. These twin sparrows, purchased by the leper, were to be identical in appearance, size, and price, and formed a single sacrifice, illustrative of the way Christ shared man's common lot in order to make atonement for the outcasts of society.

The cedar stick was cut from the most magnificent and valuable tree in Palestine. Found wherever man has traveled, the cedar remains evergreen in heat and cold, in arid wastes and on mountaintops, and defies tempest and drought alike. Famed for undecaying vitality, it symbolizes those who are "hid with Christ in God."[45] Monarch of the forest, "the cedar is repeatedly employed as an emblem of royalty and . . . to represent the righteous . . . who do the will of God."[46] Its spreading branches depict the Lord graciously overshadowing His dear subjects. Aromatic, decay-resisting, and regal, the cedar was redolent of the constancy and kindness of Christ the King.

The carmine cord, or twisted piece of fabric, has played a conspicuous role in Scripture. Made of wool, the clothing of lambs, its color was obtained from the essence of crushed cochineal spiders.[47] In salvation's story we observe that the same word is used of the piece of crimson twine which identified the first-born twin of Tamar, Judah's passing love,[48] marked for redemption the home of Rahab the harlot in cursed Jericho,[49] framed the lips of Solomon's beloved, whispering words of affection,[50] singled out the Lord's goat for death on the Day of Atonement, and for the leper's cleansing was used by the priest to tie the bunches of hyssop to the cedar stick in order to make a sprinkling instrument.[51]

Hyssop belongs to the family *labiatae*, which includes thyme, rosemary, mint, savory, marjoram, and other aromatic herbs. Its furry leaves hold liquids well. "The hyssop . . . was the symbol of purification . . . in the cleansing of the leper. . . . In the psalmist's prayer also its significance is seen: 'Purge me with hyssop, and I shall be clean: wash me, and I shall be whiter than snow.' "[52] David's word *purge* is literally "sin-offering me," and the hyssop applied the redeeming and cleansing blood. The rabbis concluded that Solomon was interested in this ritual from his allusion to "the cedar tree that is in Lebanon even unto the hyssop that springeth out of the wall."[53] The cedar's royal splendor and the hyssop's unassuming modesty point to qualities which enable the Saviour to cleanse mankind.

The earthen pot for the water typified Christ's earth-born humanity and pictured His humility in bearing in Himself the cleansing elements of life and death to the needy and defiled. It also represented His disciples, who, as "earthen vessels," should carry the purifying and redemptive gospel treasure to an unclean world.[54] This common and little-valued crock held the most vital elements, living water and sacrificial blood, for the rite of cleansing from the leprosy of sin.

Olive oil symbolized the illuminating, healing, and soothing ministry of the Spirit. The three lambs, two for sin offerings and one for a burnt offering, with its appropriate meal and wine offerings, pointed to various other aspects of the Saviour's sacrifice.

When all had been readied, the priest accompanied the leper into the country in search for a spring, and from its living water half filled the earthen jar.[55] Randomly selecting one of the sparrows, the ministrant pinched off its head with his nail.[56] His horrifying personal act of slaughter recalls the vicious treatment of the Lamb of God at the hands of His own people, from the soldiers of Herod and the mercenaries of Pilate. The terrible drama of Calvary was enacted, not by remotely controlled impersonal instruments, but by the vindictiveness of man's hands. The priest's act also typified Christ's laying down His own life, Himself the Priest, Himself the Victim.

The priest then squeezed the sparrow's blood into the water in the jar, dug a hole nearby, and buried the little body close to its place of slaughter,[57] anticipating, perhaps, Joseph's new tomb near Golgotha. Was it to this act of callous indifference that Jesus alluded in these poignant words: "Are not two sparrows sold for a farthing? and one of them shall not fall on the ground without your Father."[58] When the celestial Sparrow was cast upon the earth, His Father suffered with Him.

But this cruel death and heartless burial were not the end. The dead bird was to live on in its twin! To illustrate this, the priest caught the live sparrow by its wing tips and tail, and baptized it by immersion in the water and blood in the little earthenware font. Was it to this baptism in blood that Jesus alluded in His question to James and John, "Are ye able . . . to be baptized with the baptism that I am being baptized with?"[59] Then, turning toward the open field, the priest released the little bird to its joyous flight into the heavens, bearing its fellow's lifeblood. What an eloquent type of the atonement! "There were death and life blended, presenting to the searcher for truth the hidden treasure, the union of the pardoning blood with the resurrection and life of our Redeemer. The bird slain was over living water; that flowing stream was a symbol of the ever flowing, ever cleansing efficacy of the blood of Christ . . . the fountain that was opened for Judah and Jerusalem."[60]

The priest next dipped the hyssop into the water and blood and splashed the besom on the leper's hand, and, the rabbis add, his head, seven times.[61] "Seven" underscores the completeness of the cleansing.[62] The leper was still obliged to remain secluded from his family for a week, and then the following rites granted him full fellowship. First, every visible hair was shaved from his body.[63] These leprous gray hairs, which had evidenced his degeneracy[64] were gone! Next the leper was ritually immersed, or baptized[65] and prepared for the concluding ceremonies.

The priest offered one of the three lambs as the leper's trespass offering. Catching its blood in a vessel, the priest accompanied the leper to the door of the temple. Stationing the leper just outside, he invited him to thrust his head across the threshold into the court. Pouring some lamb's blood into his left palm, the priest dipped his finger into it and applied the blood to the leper's right ear. He then asked the leper to put his right hand into the court, and similarly bloodied his thumb, and finally his right great toe. "Finger" signals the precise and personal ministry of the Spirit.[66] This ceremony also marked the consecration of the priest. Was the Lord signaling that the leper was now a member of His "royal priesthood"?

The live sparrow, vanishing into heaven with its companion's blood, anticipated Christ's ascension to His Father, bearing our humanity and carrying with Him the merits of His sacrifice, preparatory to sending down cataracts of the Spirit's gifts. To demonstrate this enduement, the priest poured oil into his bloody palm and flicked some of it with his finger "seven times" toward the most holy place, the location of God's throne. He then invited the leper to repeat what he had done and smeared oil on the parts he had daubed with blood—his ear, thumb, and toe. This ceremony proclaimed that the cleansed leper was henceforth to listen to God's voice, work for Him, and walk along His pathway, disciplined by Calvary's sprinkled blood and Pentecost's gift of the Spirit. The priest's hand, drenched with blood and oil, was mute testimony to two vital ministries of the Saviour, sacrifice and intercession. The priest next assisted the leper in presenting his sin offering of repentance and burnt offering of consecration, with appropriate meal and wine offerings. He finally pronounced him clean in God's sight and fully restored to fellowship with his family and people.

What thoughts flood our hearts as we watch plain brown birds flitting happily here and there in our yards. Sparrows are found wherever man lives and are seen fluttering upon his roads of commerce. Costing but a farthing in Israel's ritual mart, Jesus used sparrows in both the Old and New Testaments to illustrate precious gospel truths. What man esteems of little value, indifferently flinging to the ground and burying out of sight, Heaven regards as precious. To arrest our attention, Christ wrote the story of salvation's cleansing power in the life and death, resurrection, and ascension of a homely brown sparrow! The implication of His "autobiography," embedded in the ritual laws covering leprosy, Israel might have understood, if it had studied them reverently and humbly. But the people indifferently flung the Sparrow to earth, crushed by vengeful fingers, and only the Father really cared. Now the Sparrow asks wistfully, "Is it nothing to you, all ye that pass by?"[67] Our hearts should joyfully respond, "All my *cleansing* is Christ's."

Postscript to Leviticus

We have come to the end of our trip through Leviticus and have found that its types and symbols have compelled us to look into the face of Christ. And as we have gazed on Him through the lens of the ceremonial laws, we have longed to become more and more like Him.

In the burnt offering we have seen His total commitment to His Father's will and found in it a measure of what our own dedication should be.

In the meal and drink offerings we have looked at the fullness of Christ's self-renunciation in willingly laying all He once enjoyed upon the altar of service and sacrifice.

Through the peace offering we have been warmed by His gracious invitation to join Him in covenant fellowship and to feast upon His "body and blood" in quiet restfulness.

In the sin/trespass offering we have noted how Jesus bore our sins and guilt on the altar and by His sacrificial blood paid the ransom for our souls. We have watched the priest record our confessed and forever forgiven sins in the sanctuary and thought of Jesus in the heavenlies.

And on the Day of Atonement we have followed our High Priest, reaffirming His forgiveness of our past sins and removing their records forever from our sight and His, assuring us that He will vindicate His own before the Father and the watching universe.

Through the regulations governing the call, consecration, and conduct of the priesthood, we have traced the steps which the Son of God took to become the Priest and High Priest of the heavenly sanctuary. We watched Him strip off His royal robe and kingly crown so that He might take man's likeness to meet him where he was, and lift him to where the Father designed he should be.

The annual feasts helped us to survey God's control of the crucial epochs of salvation history. By them we reviewed Christ's fulfillments of all the types which point to crises in His life and ministry, and have seen how accurately they occurred at the precise times indicated. We have observed how these festivals have covered man's pilgrimage from Christ's Paschal redemption, through the Spirit's Pentecostal empowering, and on to the rest of the Father's harvest home. Our hearts have thrilled with the realization that they look beyond time to the newly organized earth resettled with emancipated people freed from all debts, living forever in sabbatical rest to praise and glorify God in the final Jubilee.

We concluded our survey by considering the way in which the sacrifice of Christ removes from leprous humanity the corruption of sin, so shatteringly defined by the legislation contained in Leviticus. Christ's amazing sacrifice, pictured in the cruel slaughter of a vulnerable and defenseless sparrow, helped us to sense His humility and condescension and the all-embracing results of His death. And throughout our study we have felt again and again that as the Author and Finisher of our salvation, *CHRIST* IS ALL!

Notes and Sources

Introduction to Leviticus

1. Lev. 25:32, 33
2. Matt. 8:4; Luke 5:14; cf. Lev. 14:1-32
3. 6T 392
4. Num. 1:1; 10:11

Part I—Sacrifices and Offerings

Preview

1. Ps. 40:6-8; Heb. 10:4-10
2. Eph. 5:2
3. Eph. 1:6
4. 1 John 4:17
5. Ps. 40:7, 8
6. Heb. 10:5, margin of some Bibles
7. Eph. 5:2
8. Eph. 5:27; cf. Num. 28:3; 29:29
9. 1 Sam. 15:22; Hosea 6:6; Ps. 50:8-14
10. Ps. 40:5-8
11. Heb. 9:22
12. Lev. 17:11
13. Zech. 13:1; cf. John 19:34; 1 John 5:5, 6
14. Eph. 5:26; Titus 3:5
15. Heb. 4:12-15
16. Acts 22:16
17. Lev. 1:9
18. Mal. 3:2, 3; Isa. 4:4
19. Lev. 9:24

Chapter 1—The Whole Burnt Offering

1. 2 Chron. 29:27; *Tamid* 7:3
2. *Korban* Lev. 1:2
3. *Olah* Deut. 33:10; Psalm 50
4. *Kalil* only in Deut. 33:10; Ps. 51:19
5. Cf. Lev. 6:22, 23; 1 Sam. 7:9
6. Cf. John 12:3
7. Lev. 1:2, 3, 10, 14; 14:4, margin
8. Prov. 14:4
9. Ps. 144:14, margin
10. Deut. 33:17
11. Isa. 53:7
12. Gen. 3:10
13. Matt. 10:16
14. Isa. 38:14; 59:11
15. Lev. 1:15, margin
16. Num. 28:10, 15, 24, 31
17. Ex. 29:38-46
18. John 6:44; 12:32
19. Lev. 1:3, 4, NKJV; the Hebrew translated "voluntary will" in v. 3, is more precisely rendered "accepted" in v. 4 and elsewhere, cf. Lev. 22:21
20. Lev. 11:1-8
21. Lev. 1:3; 22:19, 21-25
22. Lev. 1:3; 22:19-24; John 14:30
23. Rom. 12:1
24. Lev. 22:21
25. Lev. 1:11

26. *Middoth* 3:5
27. Ps. 118:27
28. Ps. 118:27
29. Lev. 1:4; *Menahoth* 9:8
30. Matt. 26:39
31. DA 742
32. 1 Pet. 5:7
33. Quoted by A. Edersheim,
    The Temple, p. 114
34. Rom. 3:25
35. Cf. Josh 5:9, margin
36. Lev. 1:5, 11
37. Lev. 1:15, margin
38. John 10:15, 7
39. *Middoth* 3:5
40. Lev. 7:8
41. Gen. 3:21
42. Rev.19:7, 8
43. Lev. 1:12
44. Deut. 12:21
45. Deut. 12:21; Hullim 1:1, n. 7
46. Zech. 13:1
47. 2 Tim. 2:15
48. *Loutron,* from the same root as
    the LXX *loutera,* Eph. 5:26;
    Titus 3:5
49. *Hullin* 7:1
50. Gen. 32:25, 32
51. *Middoth* 3:1, 3
52. Lev. 1:5; "scattered,"
    Ezek. 10:2
53. Lev. 17:11
54. *kafar*
55. Rev. 5:6
56. DA 439
57. 4T 319
58. 3T 559
59. Lev. 2:13; Num. 18:19;
    2 Chron. 13:5
60. Lev. 3:11, 16; 21:17, margin
61. Lev. 1:8, 9
62. *yaqar,* cf. Isa. 43:4
63. "good" in KJV, Gen. 45:18;
    Isa. 43:4
64. Matt. 22:37
65. Eph. 5:2
66. 1 John 4:17
67. Lev. 1:7; Gen. 22:9
68. Lev. 1:8
69. PP 348
70. *Tamid* 2:3
71. DA 581; 5T 146
72. Gal. 4:4
73. Cf. Matt. 5:25, 26
74. Luke 23:46
75. Eph. 1:6
76. *anabaino,* John 20:17;
    Eph. 4:8, 10
77. *anphero,* Luke 24:51; Heb. 7:27
78. Job 5:7
79. Lev. 1:9, 13, 17
80. Gen. 8:21, margin
81. Gen. 2:1-3
82. Ruth 1:8, 9
83. Matt. 11:28-30
84. Eph. 5:2
85. Isa. 53:11
86. Gen. 22:2
87. 2 Chron. 20:7;
    James 2:21-23
88. Gen. 22:13
89. John 8:56

Chapter 2—The Meal/Drink Offerings

1. Lev. 2:1; Num. 15:2-19
2. *Menahoth* 4:3
3. *Korban*
4. Lev. 2:1
5. Gen. 4:3, 4
6. Gen. 32:13-21

7. Gen. 43:11
8. *Menahoth* 10:7
9. *hallah* 1:1; 3:7, 10; 4:3
10. *Menahoth* 13:1
11. John 12:24
12. Mark 4:28
13. Isa. 28:28; cf. 53:5
14. *Menahoth* 6:7
15. Mark 9:19
16. Lev. 2:4; *Terumoth* 11:3
17. *Menahoth* 6:3
18. Acts 10:38
19. Luke 1:35
20. Heb. 9:14; 1 Pet. 3:18
21. Luke 4:18; Eph. 5:23;
    Gal. 5:22-26
22. 2 Pet. 1:4
23. Acts 1:5-8
24. Lev. 2:13; Mark 9:49
25. Lev. 2:1, 2, 15, 16; 24:7;
    Num. 5:15
26. PP 353
27. Cant. 1:3
28. Ps. 45:7, 8
29. Lev. 1:11, NEB
30. See chapter 7 for "leaven"
31. Lev. 2:11, cf. "date honey"
    Terumoth 10:2, 3
32. Prov. 25:27
33. 1BC 721
34. Lev. 23:17
35. *Menahoth* 5:2; Lev. 2:11
36. John 4:10
37. *challah,* Lev. 2:4
38. The same word is used in
    Leviticus and Ps. 109:22.
39. Zech. 12:10; cf. John
    19:33-37; Ps. 22:16
40. Gen. 15:17; Isa. 31:9
41. Ps. 21:9
42. Cf. Eph. 6:16; 1 Peter 4:12
43. Lev. 2:5, margin
44. Lev. 2:7, 8
45. Only found in Psalm 45:1,
    margin
46. *Menahoth* 5:8
47. Lev. 2:14
48. Isa. 53:5, margin
49. Lev. 2:13-16
50. Ps. 20:1-3; Acts 10:4
51. Lev. 2:3, 10; 7:9-11; 10:12, 13
52. *Menahoth* 1:2
53. Lev. 2:9
54. With incense, shewbread,
    and sin offering
55. 1BC 739
56. EGW 6BC 1078
57. *gam*
58. Abel's *mincah* specifically
    mentioned twice
59. *Menahoth* 4:3
60. EGW 1BC 1086
61. Num. 15:4-11; 28:7-15;
    Lev. 23:18
62. Lev. 23:13; Num. 28:7
63. *Terumoth* 11:3
64. *Menahoth* 9:6; cf. Num. 15:3
65. Deut. 32:14
66. Num. 15:5-7
67. Ex. 30:9; Hos. 9:4
68. Num. 28:7
69. Isa. 25:7; 30:1;
    Num. 4:7, margin;
    Ex. 25:29, margin
70. Deut. 32:36, 38
71. Lev. 3:17; 7:23-27
72. Gen. 49:11
73. Lev. 2:11, NEB
74. *SDA Source Book,* 122-124
75. *Berakoth* 8:2;
    Peashim 10:2, 4, 7
76. John 19:34-37;
    DA 772
77. EGW *Signs,* August 29, 1878

78. Gen. 35:9, 10
79. Gen. 35:11, 12
80. Gen. 17:1-21
81. Gen. 26:2-5
82. *nasak*
83. *yatsaq*
84. Gen. 35:14
85. *nasak*
86. 1 Chron. 11:19, 18
87. *Pseudomai,* 2 Tim. 4:6, Berkeley
88. middle voice
89. often hophal or
    causative passive
90. Phil. 1:20-22; 1 Cor.
    15:31; Rom. 12:1
91. *hoti*

92. Phil. 2:17
93. *Analusis,* 2 Tim. 4:6
94. Col. 1:24
95. *nasak*
96. Prov. 3:19; 8:1, 23,
    "set" for *nasak*
97. Rev. 4:11
98. Ps. 2:1-5; cf. Acts 4:25-28
99. Ps. 2:6, "set" for *nasak*
100. Bullinger's suggestion
101. Ps. 2:8
102. Rev. 5:9, 10
103. Rev. 5:6; the perfect
    indicates continuing
    results
104. Heb. 10:5-10

Chapter 3—The Peace Offering

1. Josh. 11:19
2. Hos. 9:15; 10:1, 4
3. Num. 25:12; Isa. 54:10
4. Deut. 20:12, 13; 1 Kings 22:44
5. Lev. 3:17; 23:14, 21, 31
6. Num. 15:8, NEB
7. Ps. 50:10
8. Rev. 3:20
9. Pss. 51:17; 54:6; 116:17-19
10. *zabach*
11. "kill," Deut. 12:15, 21; etc.
12. Lev. 11:1-47; 17:1-16
13. Deut. 12:1-21
14. the "command" deduced
    from Deut. 12:21;
    Hullim 1:1, note 7
15. DA 660
16. Gen. 15:9-18; cf. Jer. 34:18, 19;
    Ps. 50:5
17. Heb. 10:5-10
18. John 6:63
19. Lev. 3:1, 6, 12
20. Lev. 3:2, 8, 13

21. Lev. 3:2, 8, 13
22. Quoted by Edersheim,
    op. cit. p. 117
23. Lev. 7:17, 11, 30-34;
    cf. 1 Sam. 2:12-17 for
    an abuse of this
24. Lev. 7:2-5
25. Num. 18:8, 11, 19; Lev. 7:32
26. Lev. 7:30, 34
27. Lev. 2:2, 9; 7:32, 33;
    10:15; *Menahoth* 5:6
28. Lev. 3:11; 21:6, 8, 21, 22;
    22:25; Mal. 1:7, 12
29. Mal. 1:12
30. Lev. 3:1-5; 1:7-9; 6:21
31. 1 Kings 18:24, 38; Heb. 12:29
32. Deut. 33:12
33. Cant. 8:6
34. Lev. 3:5, 16
35. Lev. 7:11-14
36. Num. 15:3-12
37. Lev. 7:11
38. John 6:48

39. Deut. 12:18; 16:11
40. Luke 14:12-14
41. Lev. 7:31
42. Lev. 10:14, 15
43. Lev. 7:31
44. Lev. 22:3-7; 7:19, 21
45. Lev. 7:11-21
46. Lev. 7:12, 13, 15; 22:29; Ps. 119:108
47. Ps. 50:7-15
48. Ps. 116:12-19
49. Pss. 51:17; 54:6; 56:12
50. Heb. 13:12-15
51. Amos 4:4, 5; 5:22, margin
52. Ps. 107:21, 22
53. Lev. 7:11-19; 9:4; Ps. 130:4; 2 Chron. 29:31
54. Ex. 3:16-22; 5:3
55. Isa. 53:5
56. Isa. 52:7; Eph. 6:15, 19, 20
57. Rom. 5:9, 10
58. Eph. 6:23; etc.
59. Phil. 4:7; Col. 3:15
60. Lev. 22:21-23
61. Lev. 7:12, 13
62. Amos 4:5
63. Lev. 7:16; Pss. 56:12; 76:11; 116:14; Isa. 19:21
64. Deut. 12:17-19
65. Lev. 7:16, 18
66. See Lev. 27:1-34
67. Num. 30:2
68. Psalm 15:4
69. Acts 5:1-11; cf. *Nedarim* 1:1, note 1
70. Num. 6:13-18
71. Acts 21:23-27
72. Gen. 31:49-55
73. Ps. 50:5
74. Eph. 2:14
75. John 14:27
76. Ps. 119:165
77. Rom. 5:1
78. Col. 1:21, 22; 2 Cor. 5:18
79. Isa. 48:18

Chapter 4—The Sin Offering

1. 1 John 3:4
2. Rom. 3:23
3. Rom. 14:23
4. James 4:17
5. Rom. 6:23
6. PP 68, 71; Gen. 3:15, 21; 4:3, 4
7. Ex. 29:10-14
8. 1 Cor. 2:14; John 3:19
9. Luke 23:34
10. Acts 7:60
11. 1 Tim. 1:15
12. a *male* animal, cf. Lev. 4:2, 3
13. 2 Cor. 5:21, cf. 14, 15; Eph. 5:2
14. Prov. 8:36, 15, 16
15. Judg. 20:16
16. Prov. 19:2
17. 2 Chron. 29:24
18. Ex. 29:36
19. Lev. 8:15
20. Ps. 51:7
21. Lev. 4:2-4
22. Ps. 50:10
23. Lev. 5:5; Num. 5:6, 7
24. Cf. Lev. 16:21; Isa. 53:4, 5
25. Lev. 4:5-7
26. AA 585
27. Lev. 4:7
28. Lev. 4:4-7, 16-18
29. Heb. 8:1-3; 4:14-16; 7:24-26; 9:12
30. Lev. 4:7, 18, 25, 30, 34
31. Lev. 4:25, 34

32. Lev. 4:11, 12, 21; 6:30; Ex. 29:14
33. Heb. 13:11-13
34. Lev. 4:8-10, 19
35. Heb. 13:12
36. Lev. 6:25, 26, 29; 10:18; 14:13
37. *Hallah* 1:8
38. Cf. Lev. 2:12
39. Lev. 4:6
40. Lev. 4:6
41. 1 Kings 9:25

42. *Zebahim* 5:1, 2
43. *Menahoth* 3:6, emphasis and explanations mine
44. Rabbi Eliezer ben Jose, *The Babylonaian Talmud, Yoma* 57a, p. 266, emphasis mine
45. 3SP 166, 167, emphasis mine; *Shekalim* 8:5

Chapter 5—The Day of Atonement

1. GC 418
2. Lev. 23:27-32
3. Heb. 10:3, Moffatt
4. Lev. 16:19, 30
5. Lev. 23:29
6. *Rosh haShannah* 1:2
7. Henry Daniel-Rops, *Daily Life in the Time of Christ,* p. 397; Josephua, *Antiq.* III:10:3
8. *Treasures of the Talmud,* p. 97
9. Lev. 16:31
10. Bow down or humble self, Ps. 35:13; 69:10
11. Lev. 16:29, 31; 23:27, 32
12. Jer. 36:6
13. Isa. 58:3-7; cf. CD 90 for a definition of true fasting
14. Joel 2:15-27; 3:11-17
15. Heb. 10:25
16. Rev. 14:7
17. Dan. 8:14
18. Cf. Lev. 16:3, 5; Num. 29:11; *Yoma* 3:4
19. Heb. 7:25; 4:15, 16
20. Lev. 16:4; *Yoma* 3:6
21. *Kenosis,* Phil. 2:5-9
22. EGW RH, June 15, 1905

23. DA 25
24. Lev. 16:6; cf. 4:3
25. *Yoma* 3:8, "his bullock"
26. *Yoma* 3:9
27. Lev. 16:8, margin
28. Cf. Ps. 16:5, a Day of Atonement psalm; Isa. 17:14
29. *Yoma* 4:2
30. Acts 2:23
31. *Yoma* 4:2
32. *Yoma* 4:3
33. *Yoma* 5:1
34. Lev. 16:17
35. *Yoma* 5:1
36. Heb. 9:4
37. *Yoma* 5:1
38. PP 353
39. John 17:1-26
40. Heb. 5:7
41. Lev. 16:6; *Yoma* 1:1
42. 2 Cor. 11:2; Eph. 5:23
43. EGW 5BC 1133
44. *Yoma* 5:3
45. *Menahoth* 3:6; *Yoma* 5:3
46. Rev. 5:6
47. *Yoma* 5:3
48. Matt. 3:13-17

49. John 1:29, 36
50. John 12:28-30
51. John 20:17
52. 3SP 202, 203
53. L. S. Chafer, *Systematic Theology, VII*, p. 20, emphasis mine
54. *Zebahim* 5:1, 2, emphasis mine; *Menahoth* 3:7; *Yoma* 5:4
55. Lev. 16:18; Ex. 30:10; *Yoma* 5:5, 6
56. Lev. 16:18, 19
57. *Yoma* 5:6
58. Lev. 16:20, 33
59. J. Morgenstern, "Scapegoat," *An Encyclopedia of Religion*, p. 69
60. *kafar*
61. Acts 3:19; Dan. 7:10; Rev. 22:11; 20:12
62. Lev. 23:20; Ex. 32:33; Rev. 3:5; Ps. 69:28
63. Cf. Lev. 16:6, 10, 16, 17 twice, 18, 19, 20, 24, 27, 30, 32, 33 twice, 35 twice
64. *taher*
65. Lev. 16:19, 30, 34 twice
66. Job 4:17
67. *taher* used in Lev. 16:30
68. M. Kalisch, *Commentary on the Old Testament*, II, p. 211
69. *Yoma* 8:9
70. *lamed* as a prefix
71. *Manuel of Biblical Archaeology*, II, p. 44
72. Lev. 16:26

73. Lev. 17:11
74. Lev. 16:10
75. Luke 8:31
76. James 2:19
77. Rabbi Ahitur, *Encyclopedia Judaica*, III, p. 1002, art. "Azazel"
78. Rev. 20:1, 2; cf. Lev. 16:21
79. 2 Pet. 2:4; Jude 6
80. Isa. 14:16, 17
81. Lev. 16:25, 27; Heb. 13:11-13; *Yoma* 6:7
82. *Yoma* 7:3
83. Lev. 16:3, 24
84. *Yoma* 7:3
85. *Yoma* 7:4
86. Cf. Rev. 15:8
87. Cf. Rev. 8:3-5
88. *Shekalim* 8:5; *Yoma* 5:1, "one curtain," 3SP 166, 167
89. Heb. 10:20
90. Cf. Dan. 8:14, RSV
91. Lev. 25:9
92. Num. 6:23-27
93. Ps. 89:15; EW 280
94. Ps. 50:5
95. EW 286
96. EW 286
97. *Yoma* 7:4
98. Rev. 19:9
99. John 15:15

Part II—The Priesthood

Preview

1. Psalm 96:9, margin

Chapter 6—The Priest and High Priest

1. Num. 5:11-31; Deut. 17:8-13; 19:17
2. Heb. 5:5, 6
3. Heb. 5:1
4. Heb. 2:14-18
5. Heb. 7:11-19
6. Ezra 2:61, 62
7. Ex. 19:5, 6
8. Mal. 2:7
9. Ex. 32:19, 20, 26
10. Num. 3:45
11. Num. 8:11-19; 3:6-13
12. Ps. 106:16
13. Num. 18:7; Ex. 28:1
14. Num. 4:3; cf. 8:24; 1 Chron. 23:3, 24, 27
15. Ezek. 34:8, 12-16
16. Num. 16:1, 3-50
17. Heb. 5:4-6
18. Lev. 21:17-23
19. Ex. 28:36
20. Lev. 21:7, 8
21. 2 Cor. 11:2
22. Ps. 16:3-6
23. Matt. 8:20
24. Lev. 8:1-36
25. Ex. 4:16; 18:19; Deut. 5:5
26. Ex. 28:2
27. See Rev. 7:14, "made white"
28. GW 173
29. Rev. 19:8
30. 1 Peter 1:13; Heb. 7:9, 10; Ezek. 1:26, 27
31. Ex. 28:39
32. Eph. 6:14; 2 Sam. 22:40
33. Ex. 28:4, 36-39
34. Ex. 28:31-35
35. Ezek. 1:16
36. Num. 15:37-40
37. Lev. 10:6; Ex. 39:23
38. Heb. 10:20
39. Ex. 28:35
40. Ex. 28:6, 12
41. Gen. 49:15; Isa. 9:6; Deut. 33:12
42. Ex. 39:5; 29:5
43. Rev. 1:13
44. Ex. 28:15
45. PP 351
46. Num. 2:1-34
47. Gal. 3:16
48. Ev. 379, 380
49. 1T 705
50. Rev. 5:9
51. Mal. 3:17
52. PP 351
53. Ex. 39:30
54. Lev. 21:12; 8:12; Ex. 29:7
55. Ps. 133:1-3
56. Lev. 8:22, 23
57. Lev. 8:23, 24
58. Lev. 8:25-28; Ex. 28:41, margin; 29:9, margin; Num. 6:7
59. Lev. 8:10, 11; Ex. 30:25-29

Part III—The Feasts of the Lord

Preview
1. GC 399
2. GC 399, 400

Chapter 7—Feasts of New Moons and Trumpets

1. Gen. 1:16; Psalm 104:19
2. MB 40
3. CT 189
4. 4T 581
5. *Rosh Hashanah* 2:5; hereinafter this will be noted as *Rosh*
6. *Rosh* 2:5-7
7. *Rosh* 2:8
8. *Rosh* 3:1
9. *Rosh* 2:7
10. Num. 10:10
11. *Rosh* 3:3
12. Job 38:7
13. Judg. 15:14
14. Ps. 65:13
15. Joel 2:1; Num. 10:7
16. Isa. 16:10
17. *Rosh* 4:9
18. Num. 10:1-10
19. Ex. 30:11-16
20. Ex. 26:19, 21, 32
21. PK 410
22. Cf. 1 Cor. 14:8
23. Hos. 8:1
24. Isa. 27:13
25. *Tamid* 7:3; *Rosh* 3:8
26. Ps. 81:3
27. Prov. 10:20
28. See Dan. 8:19; Hab. 2:3
29. PP 304
30. See Neh. 13:29; Ps. 132:1
31. Lev. 23:24
32. Num. 29:1
33. Isa. 62:6, margin
34. Acts 10:4
35. Luke 23:42
36. *Rosh* 2:2-4
37. *Rosh* 2:4
38. Lev. 23:24
39. 3T 484
40. "drove out," Gen. 3:24; cf. Gen. 21:10, 14
41. A perversion of this is seen in Jer. 44:15-19
42. 2 Kings 4:23
43. *The Jewish Encyclopedia* XII, art. "New Moon," pp. 997-1039
44. Rev. 14:4
45. Isa. 66:22, 23
46. Rev. 22:3
47. Hos. 2:11
48. 1 Sam. 20:5, 6, 29
49. 1 Sam. 20:5, 18, 24
50. Ex. 40:2, 17
51. Num. 2:34
52. Num. 3:6, 12, 13
53. Num. 33:38, 39; 20:23-29
54. 2 Chron. 29:17
55. Joel 2:1, 11-17; 1:14, 15
56. Rev. 14:1-5
57. Matt. 24:31; 1 Cor. 15:52; 1 Thess. 4:16
58. Rev. 8:2; 10:7; 11:15; 14:6; cf. Ex. 19:14-19
59. Ps. 69:28; Ex. 32:32
60. Ps. 33:15
61. *Rosh* 1:2
62. Heb. 12:19-26
63. Ps. 89:15, RV, margin
64. Rev. 21:3
65. Rev. 7:4-15
66. Isa. 66:22, 23

Chapter 8—Feasts of Passover and Unleavened Bread

1. Gen. 15:13; Ex. 12:40, 41
2. Ex. 12:3-6, 13
3. Cf. Rev. 11:8
4. Ex. 12:2
5. DA 75
6. Ex. 13:4; 23:15; 34:18; Deut. 16:1
7. Neh. 2:1; Esther 3:7
8. Lev. 23:10, 11
9. Lev. 23:9-14
10. Ex. 12:3, 6
11. John 12:1
12. Luke 19:41-48; John 12:12-15
13. DA 578
14. COS or SJ 91
15. Matt. 26:5; Mark 14:2
16. Ex. 12:6
17. Acts 4:27, 28
18. Luke 22:7, 15
19. 1 Cor. 5:7
20. Ex. 12:6, margin; *peashim* 5:1, 3; *Zebahim* 1:3; Josephus *Wars* vi:9:3
21. Matt. 26:17-29
22. John 18:28
23. Matt. 26:20
24. *Pesahim* 1:1—3:6
25. Zeph. 1:12
26. Ex. 12:18-20; 13:7; Num. 28:17
27. Ps. 119:105, margin
28. Matt. 13:33; 1 Cor. 5:8
29. Matt. 16:6-12; Mark 8:14-21
30. Luke 12:1
31. DA 409
32. Matt. 16:12
33. Acts 23:8
34. Acts 4:1-3
35. Acts 5:16-18
36. Matt. 22:23-33
37. John 11:47-50
38. Mark 8:15
39. Mark 6:14-29
40. Luke 13:31
41. Luke 23:8, "glad" in KJV
42. DA 408
43. 2 Tim. 2:19
44. Isa. 53:7, 8
45. 1 Pet. 1:19
46. Heb. 7:26
47. Isa. 53:7, 8
48. Isa. 53:5
49. Acts 8:32, 33
50. Ex. 12:4, 7, 21-23
51. 2 Chron. 30:17
52. *Pesahim* 5:5, 6
53. Prov. 4:23
54. EGW *Bible Training School,* vol. II, No. 11, April 1904
55. EGW RH, Sept. 3, 1889
56. Lev. 23:6-8
57. Josh. 24:14
58. 1 Cor. 5:6-8
59. PP 278
60. Ex. 12:11
61. Deut. 32:10
62. Num. 19:6; Lev. 14:4; PP 277
63. Ex. 12:21-23
64. *Pesahim* 5:5, 6, 10
65. PP 277
66. *Pesahim* 7:1; Ex. 12:6-8; 2 Chron. 35:13
67. Ex. 12:8, 9
68. Ex. 12:46
69. John 19:31-37
70. John 14:30; John 15:10
71. Ex. 12:8, 9
72. *zabach,* Ex. 12:27; 34:25
73. DA 389

74. PP 278
75. Ex. 12:15-17
76. EGW 2SP 276, 277
77. 1 Cor. 5:7, 8
78. PP 278
79. 2 SP 278
80. Ex. 12:8; *Pesahim* 2:6
    mentions five kinds of leaves
81. Ex. 1:14; *Pesahim* 10:5
82. PP 278
83. *Pesahim* 10:3
84. PP 278
85. Ex. 12:31-36
86. Ex. 12:13
87. John 13:23, 25

88. *Pesahim* 7:10
89. Lev. 23:10-14
90. *Menahoth* 10:1-3
91. *Menahoth* 10:4; 5:6
92. DA 785, 786;
    Matt. 16:21; 20:19
93. 1 Cor. 15:20, 23
94. Lev. 23:10, 11
95. Matt. 27:51-53
96. DA 834
97. DA 76
98. DA 672
99. Ex. 12:26, 27
100. *Pesahim* 10:8;
    1 Cor. 5:8; 11:26

Chapter 9—Feast of Pentecost

1. Ex. 23:14-17; 34:22, 23
2. Acts 20:16
3. Ex. 34:22; Deut. 16:10, 16;
    2 Chron. 8:12, 13
4. Acts 2:1; 20:16; 1 Cor. 16:8
5. Ex. 23:16
6. Num. 28:16-31
7. *Webster II,* "Shavout"
8. Deut. 16:8; cf. Ex. 12:16;
    13:6; Lev. 23:15;
    Num. 28:26
9. Ex. 19:5, 6
10. Lev. 23:15, 16; Ex. 34:22
11. AA 45
12. AA 55
13. James 1:18
14. 1 Cor. 15:20
15. John 12:24
16. Acts 2:1, 2
17. Acts 1:15
18. EGW RH, Jan. 13, 1903
19. Acts 1:8
20. 1 John 2:1
21. AA 39

22. Cf. Lev. 7:15-22; Deut. 16:9-11
23. Lev. 23:17
24. *Menahoth* 5:3
25. *Menahoth* 5:1
26. Matt. 13:33
27. EGW RH, June 10, 1902
28. 1 Sam. 1:5, margin
29. 2 Kings 2:9
30. Lev. 23:17, 18
31. Num. 28:26-31
32. Lev. 23:15-21
33. *Menahoth* 1:1; note 1; 5:6
34. 6T 366
35. Gal. 3:16, 27-29
36. Quoted by A. Ederheim,
    The Temple, p. 261
37. EGW *Signs,* March 7, 1878
38. EGW RH, Nov. 28, 1882
39. Acts 2:16, 17, "*of* My
    Spirit," only a part
40. Acts 1:14
41. Dan. 9:1-19
42. Luke 2:25-38
43. John 14:16, 17

44. Acts 1:4-8, 14
45. Zech. 10:1
46. AA 41; GC viii, ix
47. GC 611, 612; 7BC 983; Rev. 18:1
48. Ex. 40:26, 27, 34
49. 1 Kings 8:10, 11
50. Ezek. 36:25-27
51. Ezek. 36:37
52. Acts 1:14; 2:1-4
53. 2 Cor. 3:7-12
54. Heb. 12:18-21
55. Acts 2:1-4
56. Isa. 6:1-9

Chapter 10—Feast of Tabernacles

1. 2 Chron. 8:13; Ezra 3:4; Zech. 14:16-19; John 7:2
2. *hag hasuccoth*
3. Jer. 25:38; Ps. 10:9; Isa. 1:8; Jon. 4:5
4. *skene* or *skeuos*
5. 1 Pet. 3:7; Matt. 12:29; 17:4; 2 Cor. 4:7; Acts 27:17; 9:15
6. Heb. 12:9
7. Ps. 69:11; Job 36:29 2 Sam. 22:11
8. Rev. 7:15; cf. John 1:14
9. Ps. 23:6
10. A. Edersheim, *The Temple,* p. 277
11. DA 448
12. Ex. 23:16
13. DA 447
14. Deut. 16:13-17
15. Lev. 23:34-36
16. Deut. 16:14
17. Lev. 23:42
18. 1 Pet. 2:11
19. Ex. 23:16
20. Ex. 34:22, margin; Gen. 19:23
21. Job 1:21; 1 Kings 8:19; Isa. 11:1
22. 1 Kings 8:2; 2 Chron. 5:3
23. Josephus *Antiquities,* VIII:4:1
24. Deut. 16:13
25. PP 540
26. Lev. 23:35, 36
27. Ex. 25:8; A. Edersheim, *The Temple,* p. 286
28. 1 Kings 8:2; 2 Chron. 7:8
29. 2 Maccabees 10:6-8
30. John 1:14
31. Haggai 2:7; DA 23
32. Neh. 8:17
33. *Sukkah* 3:15; John 7:14
34. Deut. 31:9-13
35. Neh. 8:18
36. John 7:19
37. Num. 29:35-39; *Unger's Bible Dictionary,* p. 360
38. DA 660
39. DA 448, 449; *Sukkah* 4:9
40. Isa. 12:2, 3
41. Ps. 122:2
42. *Sukkah* 5:1, note 12
43. Ex. 17:6
44. 1 Cor. 10:4
45. Gen. 49:10
46. John 9:7
47 EGW RH, Nov. 17, 1885
48. EGW RH, Nov. 17, 1885
49. EGW RH, Nov. 17, 1885
50. DA 449; *Sukkah* 4:9
51. DA 653
52. Matt. 26:27, 28
53. Ezek. 47:1-8
54. Eph. 2:1
55. *Sukkah* 5:1
56. Deut. 16:14

57. DA 463
58. *Sukkah* 4:1-7
59. *Sukkah* 3:4-9; 4:7; cf. 23:40, "fruit of goodly trees"
60. *Sukkah* 3:8, n. 12
61. John 7:37; *Sukkah* 4:5
62. *Sukkah* 4:8
63. *Sukkah* 4:5
64. *Sukkah* 4:5
65. Matt. 21:8, 9; John 12:12, 13
66. DA 463
67. DA 448
68. DA 463
69. DA 463
70. Isa. 56:6-8
71. John 1:9
72. Isa. 9:1, 2; 60:1-5
73. John 7:2; 8:1, 2, 12
74. John 8:12; DA 463, 464
75. Gen. 1:2-5
76. Gen. 15:17, 18
77. Ex. 3:2
78. Ex. 13:21, 22
79. Ex. 33:18, 19; 34:5-7, 29, 30, 35
80. 1 Kings 18:38
81. Luke 2:9
82. Matt. 28:2, 3
83. Acts 2:3
84. Acts 12:7
85. Acts 9:3
86. Acts 23:11
87. Rev. 1:13, 14
88. PP 541
89. Zech. 14:16
90. Isa. 25:6-8
91. John 14:1-3
92. Rev. 21:23
93. Rev. 22:1, 2

Chapter 11—Sabbath of Years and Jubilee

1. Lev. 23:4-37; 25:1-4
2. Deut. 15:9
3. Deut. 15:1, 2, 9
4. Lev. 25:4
5. Lev. 25:5
6. Lev. 25:6
7. Lev. 25:2
8. Deut. 15:2
9. Lev. 25:3
10. Lev. 25:9
11. 2BC 125
12. Lev. 25:3
13. Ex. 16:4, 5
14. Lev. 25:21
15. EGW 1BC 1112
16. Ex. 23:10, 11; Lev. 25:11
17. Ex. 23:11
18. Lev. 25:6
19. Lev. 25:7
20. Ex. 9:29; Ps. 24:1
21. Lev. 19:9; 23:22
22. Lev. 25:5
23. Num. 6:2-5
24. Jer. 35:1-19
25. Lev. 25:20
26. 2 Chron. 36:16-21
27. Lev. 26:14-46
28. 2 Chron. 36:14-16
29. Josephus *Antiquities* XII:8:1; XIV:10:6; SV:1:2
30. Josephus *Wars* I:2:4; *Antiquities* XI:8:6
31. Lev. 25:6
32. Lev. 25:6
33. Deut. 8:3
34. Lev. 25:21, 22
35. Lev. 25:6
36. Lev. 25:2; 26:34, 43
37. Lev. 25:6, 23
38. Deut. 10:18, 19; 15:15; 23:7
39. Deut. 15:2-6;
40. Deut. 15:1

41. Deut 15:2, 3
42. Gen. 29:18, 27
43. Deut. 15:4
44. Prov. 11:24
45. Matt. 26:11; Deut. 15:11
46. Deut. 15:7-10
47. Deut. 15:10; 12:18;
    cf. Lev. 26:4-46
48. Deut. 15:9
49. Deut. 15:13
50. Ex. 21:5, 6
51. Lev. 25:47-55
52. Ex. 23:10-22
53. Lev. 25:20-22
54. Rom. 10:17
55. Deut. 31:12, 13
56. Matt. 11:28, 29
57. Isa. 11:10
58. Deut. 15:6
59. Ps. 104:21, 27
60. Lev. 25:9

61. Ezek. 46:17
62. Ps. 89:15
63. Lev. 25:9
64. 1 Cor. 15:52
65. From Latin *jubilare* "to
    raise a shout of joy"
66. Lev. 25:10, 11
67. PP 533, 534
68. PP 534
69. Matt. 25:34
70. Titus 3:7
71. 1 Peter 1:4
72. EW 16
73. EW 35, 286
74. Acts 3:19-21
75. Isa. 63:4
76. PP 534
77. PP 534-536
78. Cf. Rev 20:1-15
79. Zech. 3:10

Part IV—Defilement
Preview
Chapter 12—Two Sparrows and the "Issues" of Sin

1. DA 266
2. Luke 5:12-14
3. EGW *Redemption* I, 72, 73
4. Lev. chapters 13 and 14;
   Hosea for leprous hairs
5. MH 67
6. Ex. 15:26; cf. Deut. 28:27
7. *Negaim* 1:1; 4:5; 6:1
8. MH 67
9. MH 67; cf. Isa. 53:4, stroke or
   "finger of God"
10. Ex. 4:6
11. Eccl. 9:10
12. Num. 12:1-16
13. PP 386
14. 2 Kings 5:20-27
15. PK 252; 5T 123; 4T 562

16. 2 Chron. 26:4, 5, 15, 16
17. PK 304; MH 278
18. Lev. 13:1-46
19. Lev. 13:47-59
20. Lev. 14:33-57
21. Eph. 1:1-3; PP 82; 1SM 115;
    EGW 1BC 1088
22. Num. 5:3; 2 Kings 7:3-11
23. 2 Chron. 26:19-23,
    margin; cf. v. 21
24. DA 262; MH 67, 68
25. Hugh Macmillan, *Ministry of
    Nature,* 70, 71, cf. 51-59;
    Nagaim 3:7; 11:4
26. COL 311
27. Rev. 3:18
28. MH 278

29. Lev. 14:34
30. Negaim 12:4
31. John 5:22
32. DA 266
33. *Negaim* 5:4, 5
34. Matt. 16:19; John 20:23
35. Isa. 1:4-6
36. Isa. 1:5; 16:7; Jer. 5:3;
    cf. SC 47
37. John 11:1-14
38. 2 SP 229, 230
39. Rom. 8:34
40. *Negaim* 14:6; *Parah* 11:9
41. Lev. 14:10, 12-14
42. Lev. 14:4; *Negaim* 14:2;
    SDA BD article "Sparrows"
43. Matt. 10:29-31
44. Luke 12:6
45. Col. 3:3
46. PP 450; Ps. 92:12
47. W. Eving and J. Thomson,
    *Temple Dictionary of the
    Bible,* p. 706
48. Gen. 38:27-30
49. Josh. 2:15-21
50. Cant. 4:3; cf. John 19:29
    where hyssop, wine, and
    lips are used together
51. Lev. 14:4
52. PP 277; Psalm 51:7, "un-sin" or
    "un-guilt" me with hyssop
53. 1 Kings 4:33
54. 2 Cor. 4:6, 7; 1 Cor. 15:47, 48;
    Lam. 4:2
55. Lev. 14:3, 4
56. Lev. 1:15, margin
57. *Negaim* 14:1; cf. John 19:41, 42
58. Matt. 10:29
59. Matt. 20:22
60. EGW 1BC 1111
61. *Negaim* 2:4; 14:2, 3
62. AA 585
63. *Negaim* 2:4; 14:2, 3
64. Hosea 7:9; Isa. 7:20;
    Negaim 4:1
65. Lev. 14:9; *Negaim* 14:2;
    cf. Eph. 5:26; Titus 3:5
66. Luke 11:20, cf. Matt. 12:28
67. Lam. 1:12